The Ancestors and Descendents
of Robert Nathaniel McDill
and Related Families

Revised

outskirtspress
DENVER, COLORADO

Outskirts Press, Inc.
http://www.outskirtspress.com

ISBN: 978-1-4787-3619-6

Outskirts Press and the "OP" logo are trademarks belonging to Outskirts Press, Inc.

PRINTED IN THE UNITED STATES OF AMERICA

The Ancestors and Descendents of Robert Nathaniel McDill and Related Families

Bob McDill

Revised

I wish to thank the following persons:

Raymond Cloud Hunt, Louise McDill, and Laura C. Edwards for their tireless work in tracing our various family histories.

My cousin, Dan McDill, and my brother, Wayne McDill, for their longtime support and encouragement in this effort.

My daughter, Katharine McDill Stover, for her excellent work as editor.

Researcher and genealogist, Shirley Wilson, who sorted through and made sense of the stacks of material that I had collected over the decades and reconciled it all with her own vast genealogical resources. She transformed an impenetrable mess into a unified whole and provided the framework for this book.

Contents

Foreword

I first became interested in our family history when my brother, Wayne McDill, gave me a book he'd put together of old family photographs. After collecting them, he'd talked at length with our aunt, Oneida McDill Herrington, who was still living at the time. Though the pictures were old—some were damaged and all the people in them were long dead—she identified the places and subjects. Those faces captured me in some way. Had I inherited something from some of them, a nose, a chin? Or perhaps I'd inherited a deeper genetic trait like frugality or the need to always be busy? What lay hidden in those Scottish and English genes? And were there other origins that I wasn't aware of? I also wondered what events brought those people, and thus me, to the present.

My interest first led me to contact my cousin Raymond Cloud Hunt. I knew Raymond had done some work on the Cloud and Petty family histories and some preliminary sleuthing on the McDills. Even though his histories of the Clouds and Pettys were extensive, his knowledge of the McDill line was limited. I then became acquainted through correspondence with Laura C. Edwards and Louise McDill, two very fine researchers. They had already done some difficult detective work. With their help, my knowledge of our line was pushed back several generations.

As my facts, my pictures and my documents began to pile up, I saw that it all needed to be contained in a book. But I needed a model. The histories of other families that I found in the genealogy section of our library didn't satisfy me. They contained a wealth of information for sure. There were names, dates, births, deaths, land transactions, wills and lists of children. But the people in those books must have been more interesting than names and dates could tell. There were great events during their lifetimes; laws were passed, wars were fought, economies and industries rose and fell, and the New World was settled. So, in the McDill genealogy and narrative section, I relate pertinent historical markers and try to tell how they affected our progenitors. As a result, I hope the reader will gain

The Ancestors and Descendants of Robert Nathaniel McDill

a better understanding of who our ancestors were and why they did the things they did. The Callaham, Cloud and Petty genealogies contain little narrative and are primarily for the use of researchers.

The McDill sections of this book tell the history of our line and our people. It begins in Scotland in prehistory and ends in America with the death of Robert Nathaniel McDill on 25 August 1960.

—Bob McDill
Nashville, December 2012

Part One
Looking Back

The McDill Name

è

The McDill name, in that spelling, is at least 475 years old. It is a variation of the name MacDowall, spelled MacDowall, Macdowall, McDowell, MacDowell, or McDowall. As the scholar, George F. Black, tells us, "McDill is one of the many old spellings of MacDowall which has become a fixed surname."[1]

There were several branches of the Scottish MacDowall Clan, all from Galloway in Southwestern Scotland. It's difficult to say from which the McDill spelling arose. The MacDowalls, and therefore McDills, are closely related to the Highland MacDougalls and are officially members of Clan MacDougall as well as Clan MacDowall. Indeed McDill, MacDowall, and MacDougall all have the same meaning. They translate from the Gaelic MacDhughaill to mean "son of the Dane or son of the dark stranger."[2] This may refer to a Viking progenitor.

Some people believe that the "Mc" prefix indicates an Irish name and the "Mac" prefix, a Scottish one. There is some validity in this. However, many Scots in Western Scotland, and particularly in Galloway, traditionally used the "Mc" or the now rare "M'" prefix like their Irish neighbors. McDill and MacDill are virtually the same name and indicate people with the same origins. The name McDill appears in Scotland as early as 1526.

In some households, it is believed that McDill was a French Huguenot name, rendered Medill. This French connection is usually meant to explain a notion that there were no McDills in early Scotland. However, it is apparent that there were plenty of people in Scotland spelling their name "McDill" long before the French Huguenot migration in 1685. Therefore, we must accept a more traditional origin.

Tartans and Badges

℮

In a letter dated 22 February 1983, the Scottish Tartans Society informed me that there is no specific McDill tartan.[3] However, they went on to say, "As a form of MacDougall, that clan's tartans, history … are applicable for all of the name [sic] McDill, McDoll and McDull."[4] Neither was there a MacDowall tartan at the time. Since then the MacDowall Chieftain, whom I will discuss later, has created an official MacDowall tartan. The new tartan was designed over a seven-year period and was registered by the Scottish Tartans Authority on November 12, 2007. The Chief approves of not only that tartan but also three others. He states: "clansman may officially wear any of the following tartans: MacDowall (Macdowall), MacDowall-Galloway Hunting; Hunting Stewart or Galloway Hunting, and MacDougall."[5]

The issue of coats of arms is more complicated. The Lord Lyon, King of Arms tells us, "The arms, official insignia of the Chiefs, may only be used by them [sic] when recorded in the Lyon Register."[6] This means that the right to "display arms" is reserved only for those who specifically have a claim on them verified by and registered with the Court of the Lord Lyon in Edinburgh. This right is passed down from father to son and closely guarded. In other words, hanging an ancient family coat of arms on your wall, which you do not have a right to display, even though it does bear your name, is considered in veddy, veddy bad taste.

MacDowall arms are listed in *Burke's General Armory*. There are three main "stirps" or branches of the MacDowalls: Macdowall of Garthland, McDouall of Logan, and McDouall of Freugh. *Burke's* lists twelve armorial "cadets" or sub branches of these families, eleven Scottish and one Irish.[7] Some publications include the variant McDill under MacDowall of Garthland. This Coat of Arms includes "a silver lion rampant [upright], crowned gold" on a blue field.[8] The Motto is "Vincere Vel Mori" (Conquer or Die).

The Ancestors and Descendants of Robert Nathaniel McDill

The current clan Chief is "Fergus Day Hort Macdowall of Garthland, Baron of Garochloyne, Garthland, and Castlesemple, Chief of the Name and Arms of MacDowall."[9] Notice the Chief spells his name with the lower case "d." He informed me in an email that he chooses to spell his name Macdowall as it has been spelled for nine centuries, but that Clan MacDowall is spelled with the upper case "D." Concerning the Chief, the *Scottish Clan and Family Encyclopedia* tells us, "The chiefly family immigrated to Canada at the end of the 19th century. The present chief [Fergus Day Hort Macdowall] still lives in Canada, but he has reacquired some of the ancient Galloway lands, and supports clan events in this [Scotland] country."[10] Indeed the Chief has done much to revive interest in the Clan.

Then there is the matter of the crest or badge. The Lord Lyon says, "Crests, which are the emblem on the top of the helmets, encircled by a strap-and-buckle bearing the Chief's motto or slogan, may be worn as a badge by all of his name or clan."[11] In our case, this consists of a raised dagger in front of a banner containing the Latin words "Vincere Vel Mori" (Conquer or Die). This is the badge of MacDowall of Garthland. Fergus Macdowall is also Chief of MacDowalls of Castlesemple. He plans to pass that barony to his younger son David. David will then be afforded the right to use its motto, "Fortis in Arduis" (Strength in Hardship).[12]

To summarize, we have the right to wear any of four tartans and a MacDowall badge or crest. I think that's pretty generous considering our branch of the McDills left the British Isles almost two and a half centuries ago.

Branches of Clan MacDowall built at least a half dozen castles in Galloway. To my knowledge, only Machermore Castle near Newton Stewart is still standing. However, the structure was added to and remodeled in the nineteenth century and little of the original eleventh century castle remains. The Macdowalls of Machermore occupied this site until about 1600.[13] Today, the Chief's substitute "seat" is at Barr Castle in Renfrewshire. The MacDowalls acquired the lands and Castle there from the Hamilton family in 1780. All that remains of Barr Castle, however, is the central tower. [13]

Please don't think that I am trying to tie our McDills to this or any of the other chiefly or titled families of the MacDowall Clan. I am not. Even though we remain members of this clan, we are not, as far as I know, directly descended from these families. But, as you will see, much of the history of the clan is recorded through these chieftains. Therefore, they are central to the history of the McDills.

Galloway

The history of the McDills and the McDill name starts in Galloway. It was in that almost forgotten Southwest corner of Scotland that those bearing the name McDill first appeared. McDill, as we have seen, is a variation of MacDowall. The MacDowalls were the great ruling family of Galloway. The clan originally dominated a small county called Wigtown. But MacDowall lords eventually extended their power over a wider area.

Galloway is bounded on the west and south by the Irish Sea and on the north by a range of high hills. The counties of Wigtown, Kirkudbright, and Dumfries make up the region. It is dominated by a series of river valleys sloping south to the waters of Solway Firth. The southwestern tip looks across the Irish sea, only twenty-five miles from Ireland. For years, Galloway's geography set it apart from the rest of Lowland Scotland.

The People

℃

Before histories were written, Stone Age men populated the area. Later came Bronze Age and finally Iron Age inhabitants. Then in the seventh century B.C., a race from Central Europe called Celts began arriving in Britian. These people influenced and intermarried with the inhabitants of England, Scotland, and Wales, to create a people known as Britons.

That migration was followed, in the last centuries of the first millennium, by a second wave of Celtic emigrants who had inhabited an area encompassing Northeastern France, Southwestern Germany, Yugoslavia, and part of Austria. They had been forced out of Central Europe by other advancing populations. Upon their arrival in Britain, they, in turn, intermarried with the natives.

The Britons were a pagan, war-like people. They had no written language and were described by the Romans, like most races outside the Empire, as barbarians. But in Britain, they became the race of King Arthur and the origin of the stories of Lancelot, Guinevere, and Galahad. In their oral mythology, we first find the ideas of courtly love and knightly behavior. Much of what we know about those times has been pieced together from studies of the things the Britons left behind: weapons, jewels, garments, pottery, gold and silver, buildings, and chariots. We know that they were warriors by the quantity and variety of their weapons.

In Galloway, the Britons built tall towers of dry stone construction called "brochs." In swampy areas, they built "crannogs" or island forts sometimes referred to as "lake dwellings."

Historian Daphne Brooke tells us:

> *Galloway's centrality on the Irish Sea coast made its people habitual sea-farers. Their destinations were not confined to the Isle of Man, Ireland, or the Scottish firths and Western Isles. They had regular commerce with Wales, Cornwall*

and Brittany [France], and even the Loire Valley and Mediterranean ports.[15]

The Britons hunted wild animals like boar and deer and celebrated the hunt in their art. Sometimes they played games or took part in sports. There was music, dancing, singing, and possibly even theatre. They also loved poetry. It was probably not what we would recognize as poetry today, but rhythmical use of words sung in musical tones to express hopes and fears or to tell the story of a hero. They loved a feast. It was an appropriate end to a good hunt to eat and drink to the point of insensibility. Party, party, Par-tay!

Romans

In the first century A.D., the Romans, who had long controlled England to the south, moved north into Scotland bent on conquest. In the year 82, an army, under Agricola, reached Galloway. There, they built forts in order to subdue the local population and launch attacks against the Picts. The Picts were an ancient warlike people who lived far north of Galloway in the Scottish Highlands. The Romans called them Picts because they tattooed or painted their bodies. But the people in Galloway, called the Novantae by the Romans,[16] were just as warlike. One historian tells us, "The royal house of Galloway apparently also resisted the Romans . . . from these early deeds the lords charged their shield with a fierce lion royally crowned."[17]

In 122 A.D., Emperor Hadrian himself visited Britain. After looking things over, he decided that Scotland simply wasn't worth the cost in blood and treasure. Furthermore, the legions were increasingly needed at home to protect Rome itself from other barbarians, so he gave the order to pull back. The historians, Peter and Fiona Fry relate:

> And this is the year generally given as the one in which he ordered the construction of his famous wall [separating Scotland from England]. It eventually became seventy-three miles long and twelve to fifteen feet high, with mile-fortlets and towers, from the Tyne to the Solway Firth. It was intended as part of Hadrian's policy of consolidating the frontiers of the Roman Empire.[18]

Britain was cut in half and all the fierce people north of the wall had regained their independence. But the Empire was descending and the Romans were unable to effectively maintain the boundary. The Highland Picts breached the wall and continued raiding south into England. And so

The Ancestors and Descendants of Robert Nathaniel McDill

"The frontier was edged downwards [southward] so that by 400, there was no Roman presence north of York, over 100 miles [south] from the wall."[19]

Rome soon abandoned Britain altogether. Immediately, bands of Picts, the ancient enemy of the Britons, began raiding south into the Scottish Lowlands and England. The Britons appealed to Rome for aid, but the Romans were much more concerned at the time with Rome itself and the Mongol hoards of Attila the Hun.

Angles and Saxons

Since the Romans were too occupied to lend a hand, the Britons called on Angles from Denmark and Saxons from northwest Germany for help. These Germanic tribes, who began arriving in about 450 A.D., were promised land in exchange for men at arms. But the Angles and Saxons quickly saw an opportunity. Britain represented rich land and easy pickings. Once these tribes started crossing the channel, they couldn't be stopped. A protracted war broke out. The various tribes of Britons aligned themselves against the invaders. Into this ancient struggle rose a figure whose legend has survived to the present day, King Arthur. Whether partly or wholly real, it was Arthur who, according to legend, rallied his people against the invaders. In fact, at that time, Galloway was known as Coit Celidon, or the Forest of Scotland. In Arthurian tales, it was the home of Sir Galleran, one of Arthur's enemies. According to fable, Galleran's lands were at first confiscated by Arthur. Later, he was forgiven and made a member of the Roundtable. In some accounts, it was Merlin's birthplace. In others, Arthur himself ruled the kingdom.

The Anglo-Saxon invaders were, in this clash of cultures, the barbarians. The Britons had benefited from four hundred years of Roman rule. They were mostly Christian and civilized. The people of Galloway were probably less Romanized but they had notably remained Christian after the Romans pulled out. In fact, St. Ninian, a British Celtic Bishop, built a church and school for religious teachers at Whithorn, near Solway in about 400 A.D. St. Ninian sent missionaries north to convert the Picts, but his efforts failed. Converting the Picts in the Highlands wouldn't begin in earnest until Irish monks established a monastery at Iona in 557.

The Angles and Saxons, with some intermarriage, became the English race. They pushed most of the Britons out of England to the "Celtic Fringe" in Wales, Cornwall, and the outer parts of Scotland. Angles moved into Galloway in the seventh and eighth centuries. But the natives later reasserted their independence and dominance. Indeed, even after a large part of the Scottish Lowlands had succumbed, Galloway remained a stronghold of the Britons. Daphne Brooke writes:

> *[Later, in the Middle Ages,] A medieval Welch Triad recalled the three thrones of the Britons, which meant apparently the three centers of old British power that survived [which did not include the Picts in the Highlands]. One was Cornwall, one Wales, and one, the power center of the Men of the North, was Penryn Rionyt.*[20]

This Penryn Rionyt was Galloway. Brooke states: "Galloway remained an enclave of Britannic social organization, law and language, after the kingdoms of the North in Lothian, northern England and even Strathclyde itself, had passed away."[21]

Scotti

ℰ

Those same Britons from England and the Scottish Lowlands had invaded Northern Ireland as early as 400 B.C. There, they had mixed with the indigenous Celtic people and founded a new kingdom.

In the fifth and six centuries, those people (called the Scotti by the Romans, which meant raiders) came roaring back across the Irish Sea. They conquered, settled, and eventually gave the people of Scotland their name. The Scotti were a sea-going people who used "coracles," small, wickerwork, canoe-like boats, covered with skins and coated with tar. They also utilized larger craft called "curraghs," which were built of timber, covered with hides and tar, and propelled by oarsmen. The principle of kin dominated their social structure. It's possible that some of the old clan names (MacDowall according to one source) originated with them.

Leo McDowell in his excellent history of the MacDowalls, relates:

> *Colla Uais Came Erc (died 502 A.D.), the king of the Dal Riata [the Scotti], had three sons. These sons were named Fergus, Angus and Lorne Mac Erc. Angus Mac Erc claimed the Isles of Islay and Jura as tribal territory, while Lorne Mac Erc absorbed what is now known as Lorn, the seat of clan McDougall.*[22]

He goes on to say that Fergus founded his dynasty in Galloway. Thus we see the ancient connection between the MacDougalls of Lorne and the MacDowalls of Galloway. Others claim the connection was made through marriage in the female line.

On the other hand, historian Charles McKinnon states:

> *Somerled, the son of Gillebride, had three sons by his Norwegian wife, the Princess Ragnhildis, daughter of King*

The Ancestors and Descendants of Robert Nathaniel McDill

Olaf of Man—Dougal, Reginald and Angus. It is from
Duogal [sic], the eldest, that the Clan MacDougall springs.
Reginald's son Donald was the MacDonald progenitor…the
Galloway MacDowalls are said to be a Lowland branch of
this [MacDougall] undoubtedly Highland Clan.[23]

But no matter what the early MacDowall origins were, historians agree that the raiding Scotti mixed with the indigenous Britons of western Scotland and the Isles. This mixture, now called Scots, would struggle with their old enemy the Picts in the Highlands for supremacy of Scotland for three more centuries.

Scotland's First King

In about 836, Alpin, ruler of a large part of Scotland, was killed in battle. His son Kenneth MacAlpin claimed the crown. Kenneth became a great leader, uniting the land and races, even including the Picts. Historian David Ross writes:

> The kingship of the Scots was then assumed by Kenneth MacAlpin, a strong man, perhaps son of a Dal Riadan [or Riatan, i.e., Scotti] sub-chief; his previous history is obscure. In 843 Kenneth also assumed the kingship of the Picts, though it took him until 847 to eliminate his rivals. Later legend would recount an organized massacre of Pictish Chiefs, following a feast at Scone. Under previous joint Kings, the identity of the two kingdoms had been preserved. Now…Kenneth set about consolidating his two kingdoms and peoples into one. Though it was based in Pictland, the Gaelic speaking Scots held the initiative. Pictland as a political concept was obsolete…Scotland was the coming thing.[24]

When he was crowned Scotland's first King in 843, Kenneth MacAlpin or Kenneth I sat on the Stone of Destiny, an ancient rock that served as the coronation stone for all Scottish kings thereafter.

In 997, Kenneth III became king by killing Constantine III. In 1005, Malcolm II killed Kenneth. Duncan I, who followed Malcolm II, was murdered by MacBeth, one of his generals, in 1040. In 1057, Duncan's son, Malcolm III, killed MacBeth.[25] Bloody Scotland.

Vikings

❦

Then things got even bloodier. In the ninth and tenth centuries, the most famous group of invaders of all entered Scotland and Galloway. A prayer was uttered in every abbey, church, and monastery in all the British Isles. "From the fury of the Northmen, deliver us, Oh Lord!" The prayer was not answered. The scholars, Peter and Fiona Fry, tell us: "'White Gentiles,' they were called if they were the tall, almost white haired Norwegians, 'Black Gentiles' if they were golden haired, a little shorter in stature and came from Denmark."[26] We are also told, "some of the Vikings settled as far south as Galloway where they lived in harmony with the Britons (now called Scots), married their women, and founded a race of energetic and wild people called the Gallgaels from whom the name Galloway is derived."[27] The native people referred to by the Frys as "Britons" were, by then, a mixture of Briton, Scotti, perhaps Anglian, and even a little Roman. We are not told why the Vikings settled down and lived peacefully among the people of Galloway when they had burned and pillaged everywhere else. Perhaps they had finally met their match. In any event, Viking blood was added to the mix.

And thus we have the makeup of the people of Galloway or, as the Romans called them, the Novantae, meaning the "energetic ones." The region "seemed to be set apart by its very geography to be a separate territorial entity."[28] The people there would for centuries be linked, not to their land-bound neighbors, but to their sea-faring relatives in Wales, Northern Ireland, and the western coast and islands of Scotland. They "were to have a long history. In the twelfth century a Scottish charter [even] referred to them as Welch."[29]

Normans

In 1066 the Normans, another Viking people, who had earlier settled on the west coast of France, crossed the channel and invaded England. Led by William, Duke of Normandy, they defeated King Harold of England on 14 October at the Battle of Hastings. William placed himself on the English throne and seized lands and titles, granting them to his own knights.

Sixty or seventy years later, King David of Scotland, partly Norman himself, began welcoming Norman nobles into Scotland, granting them lands. By this time, Fergus, first Lord of Galloway, was sovereign of Galloway. As Daphne Brooke relates:

> So long as Fergus ruled, the Anglo-Norman landowners settling in Scotland under David's patronage, found no corresponding welcome in Galloway. The power and number of Galloway's aristocracy and fighting men left no place for the new knights. Like David, Fergus's choice was limited. He had to retain the support of his people. He had to protect Galloway from Anglo-Norman acquisitiveness and [at the same time] Gallovidian autonomy from David's claim . . .[30]

Rebellious Galloway

In the late 1100s, when King William the Lion of Scotland was again attempting to unite the country, he not surprisingly had a great deal of trouble with Galloway. Historian Fitzroy MacLean tells us:

> The Celtic chieftains of the west, [Galloway] who still enjoyed a great measure of independence, were in a state of more or less permanent insurrection against the central monarchy. Fergus, [a later one] the then ruling Prince of Galloway, had rebelled no less than three times against Malcolm [the preceding king] before retiring to a monastery. And in the reign of William the Lion, [Fergus's] sons rose again, massacring, with particular gusto, the Anglo-Norman garrisons in [neighboring] southern Scotland. It was to be a long time before this last Celtic stronghold of the southwest was finally pacified.[31]

The Clans

As mentioned earlier, one MacDowall historian says that the first Fergus had two brothers, Lorn and Angus. They supposedly spawned four tribes of Scots: the Cinel Gabran and the Cinel Comgall descended from grandsons of Fergus, the Cinel Lorn and Cinel Angus descended from the brothers of Fergus. This may be an example of the early division of Scots into clans. Clan, meaning children, was a system of tribal loyalty. Some would consider it Scotland's glory and others, the reason for its bloody history and disunity.

By the twelfth century, the clan system had given way to feudalism in much of the Lowlands. Many clan chiefs had remade themselves into feudal lords. But things changed little in Galloway. Peter and Fiona Fry state:

> . . . in Galloway, the descendants of the Gallgeals were not prepared to accept feudalism or the laws that came with it. They became restless, fearing interference with their independence, and the King [of Scotland] had to let them keep their own customs. Indeed, as late as the 1380s the Scottish King's counsel was still accepting that Galloway had its own special laws.[32]

Both societies, feudal and clan, existed side-by-side. But there must have been a great difference between the farmer ruled by a lord and the clansman who could claim he was related to the chief by blood. Historian G. S. Barrow states, "British kindreds under a recognized chief were still an important part of the social organization of Galloway and Carrick in the 14th century."[33]

The Ancestors and Descendants of Robert Nathaniel McDill

Bruce

In 1294, Edward I (Longshanks) of England declared war on France. He summoned his lords and knights in the feudal tradition, commanding them to raise fighting men. Among those summoned was Balliol, King of Scotland, whom Edward considered a weak leader and his subordinate. Balliol refused and instead made a treaty with the French. Edward, in his rage, took an Army across the border into Scotland, burning, looting, and pillaging. Balliol was forced to abdicate and Edward appointed an English viceroy to rule Scotland. Scotland was to be treated as just another English County. But as Peter and Fiona Fry relate:

> The English were blind as well as arrogant if they imagined that a great and proud people like the Scots would tolerate foreign domination so tamely and without opposition. They began to resist at once, but it was not the lords and the rich landowners who had much to lose if they were caught, but more humble gentry like William Wallace, whose family had some property in Renfrewshire. Wallace's wife had been killed and his household were assaulted by English soldiers on the rampage from the Garrison at Lanark. Wallace killed the Garrison commander in return. This was the signal for revolt. Soon he had gathered about him a small but tough and determined band of warriors dedicated to the task of driving all the English, military and civilian, out of Scotland. They lived and trained in hiding, and would suddenly spring upon an English held Castle or fortified town and take it by surprise. One after another the Castles fell.[34]

But, as you probably know, Wallace was finally betrayed by his own and handed over to the English to be executed.

When Robert the Bruce finally took up the cause, all of Scotland was not behind him. The MacDowall Clan, along with their highland cousins, the MacDougalls, sided with England and Edward I (Long Shanks). After all, there had been bad blood between the MacDowalls and Bruces for years. The Balliols of Galloway had been the Bruce's main rivals for the throne of Scotland for generations. That enmity had divided the country in two. When Robert the Bruce himself aspired to the throne, he was opposed by John Comyn. Comyn was an ally of the MacDougalls and therefore the MacDowalls. After Bruce murdered him, the animosity intensified. In 1296, "Dougal and Fergus M'douall [sic] appear on the Ragman Roll of nobles swearing fealty to Edward I of England."[35] Indeed, the lords and men of Galloway, to our everrrlastin' shame, were aligned against Bruce throughout the entire war for Scottish independence.

During the struggle, the Bruces spent part of 1306 subduing the MacDowalls. David Ross relates:

> Around this time, Robert took revenge for the losses at Tyndrum by defeating John Lorne MacDougall in the Pass of Brander which brought most of Argyll under his control. Robert's brother Edward overran Galloway and forced out the anti-Bruce Chieftain Dungal MacDowall, although he failed to take such crucial castles as Lochmaben, Dumfries and Ayr.[36]

In 1307, Bruce's brothers, Thomas and Alexander, landed an army on the Galloway coast. John Prebble writes:

> They were quickly captured by a MacDowall Chief and taken to Lanercost, where Edward as quickly dispatched them. Alexander, the brilliant scholar of Cambridge, was hanged. The boy Thomas was lifted up on a gibbet. Before this he was dragged through Carlisle by a team of horses.[37]

Bruce finally subdued Galloway. After years of bitter warfare, he had united Scotland. Long Shanks was never able to realize his dream of conquering Scotland. He died in 1307, on his last campaign, within sight of the Scottish border. His deathbed command to his son Edward II was to continue the war. But Edward II was no Long Shanks. He was defeated by Robert the Bruce at Bannockburn in 1314, by an army one-third the size of his own. After Bannockburn, Edward II demonstrated that he had no taste for war. He called his knights home. Bruce had finally driven out the English and united the Scottish people under one king. Well, almost all the Scottish people were united. Historian Ronald Scott tells us:

> The problem of rewarding those who had supported him [Bruce] from the earliest years, without disturbing existing landowners . . . was happily resolved by having at his disposal lands forfeited by a small group of irreconcilables: the Earl of Atholl, John Balliol, John Comyn of Badenoch, John Comyn, Earl of Buchan, John Macdougall and Dugald Macdowall. From these estates and the royal demesne he was able to make munificent grants to his two outstanding lieutenants, Thomas Randolph and James Douglas . . .[38]

We also find that, after the war, "Dugald Macdowall's family fled to England where they were granted a manor by Edward."[39] It seems the fighting men who were left back in Galloway received no reward for their opposition to Bruce. But later the MacDowalls would side with Scotland as comrades in battle with Robert's son and heir, King David II.[40]

Two Races

By the 1400s, the separation of the two races, Anglo-Saxon and Celtic, was becoming more distinct. Galloway, due to its isolation, stubborn independence, and perhaps long association with Northern Ireland remained Celtic. Historian David Ross writes:

> The cultural gap between Highlands and Lowlands was steadily widening. Scots [the English language of Scotland] was now almost the universal tongue of the towns, low-lying countryside and the East Coast. Gaelic speech survived only in pockets. Eastern and southern Scotland, in spite of all the remnants of a Celtic way of life were also consciously part of the modernizing of Western Europe. In the Highlands and Islands, where Gaelic was their only language, people were aware that they were not part of the wider and expanding culture. With Galloway and Ireland, they were readouts of an older civilization. They were numerous enough for this to be a matter of pride rather than anxiety. In some ways their lives were influenced by new ideas imported from the continent and the world beyond. But despite the continuing high levels of achievement in the oral arts no one beyond the Celtic world took an interest in their culture.[41]

It would be some time before the two cultures in Britain became one people. Many claim they are still separate.

The Battle of Flodden

Clan MacDowall numbers were reduced appreciably in 1513. In that year, King James IV, after an appeal from the French King, decided to honor the "auld alliance" between France and Scotland. England and France were at war at the time, and James believed that by invading England he could draw English forces away from the front in France. He was a popular King and easily assembled a Scottish Army of 20,000 men. The Army met an English force led by the Earl of Surrey near Branxton on September 9. Fergus Macdowall and William MacDougall relate:

> *The ensuing battle of Flodden was lost, together with the lives of James IV and the flower of Scotland's nobility. A still higher proportion of the Galloway baronage was lost, including Uchtred Macdowall of Garthland and his son Thomas, Charles McDouall [sic] of Logan, Gilbert McDouall [sic] of Freugh and most of their male relations.*[42]

The English suffered heavy losses. But Scottish casualties numbered between five and ten thousand. It was said that the slaughter struck every farm and household in lowland Scotland.

For the men of Galloway, opposing England became a habit. Later, John MacDowall led a force against the English at Pinkie Cleugh in 1547. He was defeated by the Duke of Somerset who had earlier invaded Scotland to force submission after the death of Henry VIII. "We can speculate that the MacDowalls were among the Earl of Home's lightly armed horsemen, long characteristic of Galloway arms."[43]

First Appearance

Even though Fergus McDuhile appeared as a "juror at Berwick in Wigton in 1296," and "Gilbert Macduyl was archdeacon of Sodor before 1460,"[44] the surname first appears in the "McDill" spelling in 1526. In that year, "John McDill and Michael McDill were accused of murder as followers of the Earl of Cassilis."[45] Records indicate that, at their hearing, John and Michael McDill were "granted a continuance." In 1589, we find that "William M'Dill, son of Andrew M'Dill, Burgess of Perth, was charged in Perth with playing at the Butts." I understand this means he was caught practicing archery during preaching. Furthermore, "David M'Dill and Johnne M'Dill were witnesses in Keiris in 1619. Andrew M'Dill was a witness in the Earldom of Carrick in 1650. John M'Dill was in Largs, parish of Urr, in 1641, and Andrew McDill was charged with being a disorderly person [religious nonconforming] in the parish of Carsfern in 1684."[46]

All these early McDill sightings, with the exception of the one at Perth, are in the southwest corner of Scotland. It's easy to see that these McDills hadn't strayed far from their MacDowall Clan origins in Galloway.

It appears the first census record available for Scotland was taken in 1841. That census reveals that by then, most McDills lived in the counties of Kircudbrightshire and Ayrshire, both part of old Galloway. There were also some McDills residing in Wigtownshire, the neighboring county to the west, which was also part of old Galloway. By 1901, the largest number of McDills could be found in Ayrshire with a significant number still residing in Kircudbrightshire.[47]

The Ancestors and Descendants of Robert Nathaniel McDill

Scotland in 1600

In 1600, Scotland was a difficult place. In *The Scotch-Irish: A Social History*, James Leyburn writes: "Life everywhere was insecure, not only because of the recurrent wars with the English, but even more because of abominable economic methods, a niggardly soil, and constant cattle raiding and feuds."[48] In the southwestern Lowlands, soil was thin. There were stony moors covered with heath, long stretches of bog and moss in the lower areas, and gravelly soil along the coast. What once had been a forested region was now practically treeless. For heat, the Lowlanders burned turf, peat, and coal. Destruction of the forests had led to the extermination of wild game. Farming methods were primitive and the strains of oat and barley seed used produced very low yields. Land holdings were often rotated among tenants leaving little incentive to build and improve. The farmer was at the mercy of the landowner in more ways than one. David Ross writes:

> *Tenant farmers rented their lands in turn from the "baron," who often held the land on behalf of the greater Lord or sometimes directly of [sic] the Crown. These smaller barons were cadets of the noble families or, near Edinburgh in particular, prosperous lawyers or officials. The barony functioned as a miniature state in some respects. A large barony would have its own law court where the baron interpreted the laws of the land as he understood them.*[49]

Furthermore, as Leyburn tells us: "Like other warriors of earlier times, Scots felt the raising of cattle more manly than the raising of crops."[50] This was probably a further hindrance to prosperity. A Scottish poet of the time put it this way:

Had Cain been Scot, God had ne'er changed his doom,
Not made him wonder, but confined him home.[51]

The whole country was practically without law. Leyburn states:

> *The root of the trouble was political, for no king since*
> *the time of Robert Bruce, (d.1329) had been able to keep*
> *the English out, or rule the whole country and so provide*
> *national law and order. Scotland had no standing army, no*
> *regular taxation, no police force and very few civil servants.*
> *Under such conditions every baron was a law unto himself.*[52]

Warring families carried out vendettas against each other. Stealing a neighbor's cattle and sheep was a popular pastime. In the southwest, these feuds were especially violent and ongoing. The Montgomerys, Cunninghams, and Kennedys and their lists of opponents kept the region in a constant state of warfare. Philosopher Thomas Hobbs' often-misused phrase describing people without laws or civil society might have been applied to Scotland in the 1600s, when he wrote, "and the life of man, solitary, poor, nasty, brutish, and short."[53]

It was the farmer or herdsman who did most of the fighting. He was obligated to take up arms when his lord or chief called, whether it was against England or a neighboring clan. Unlike the barons and knights, he could not afford expensive armor. The ordinary soldier carried a wooden shield covered with animal skin, a long pointed spear, sometimes a battleaxe, a small sword, and a knife. Leyburn finds the Scottish temperament hard to understand. He states: "The curious point must be made, however, that the humble farmer, who suffered most, did not attribute his calamities to the noblemen and lairds. He seems to have regarded violent lawlessness as simply the way of the world."[54]

Needless to say, many young Scots sought their fortunes elsewhere. The poverty of the land and the dislike of the people for trade and manufacturing led many into foreign military service. They became permanent fixtures in most of the armies of Europe. For example, by 1600, there had been a Scot's Brigade in the Dutch army for two hundred years.

The Ancestors and Descendants of Robert Nathaniel McDill

The Kirk

ॐ

John Knox had brought the Protestant Reformation to Scotland in the 1560s. The Scottish branch of the Catholic Church had been one of the most corrupt, and religious reform in the form of Presbyterianism had been welcomed. By 1567, Queen Mary, a Catholic, was forced to give up the Scottish throne in favor of her infant son James. Mary, Queen of Scots, as she was later called, was imprisoned in the tower of London and finally beheaded by Queen Elizabeth I, who feared her as a rival. But upon Elizabeth's death in 1603, Mary's son James assumed the throne of both England and Scotland. James I (of England; VI of Scotland) had been raised a Protestant. During his reign, he helped to firmly establish the Presbyterian Church in Scotland.

Until the Reformation implanted a zeal for education among the Scots, schools had been few. Even though Scotland could claim three universities by 1500, there were few educated men. The universities were, for the most part, seminaries, and their graduates were almost wholly channeled into the Catholic Church. Most of the people were illiterate. The Presbyterian Church set out to establish elementary schools in every parish. From that time forward, Scotland would maintain an enthusiasm for learning. The historian John Prebble tells us, "In every parish there should be a school master, able at least, to teach Latin and grammar. In small and remote parishes where such a man might not be available, the minister or reader of the Kirk was to give the elementary instruction."[55]

Reivers

The reign of James VI brought other benefits. As king of both Scotland and England, he was able to restore peace and order for the first time in centuries. The constant wars between the two countries ended. Brigands, cattle thieves, and outlaws were no longer able to escape across the Scottish-English border, but were returned to local authorities on either side to face punishment. Continuing what James V before him had started, he sent armed forces to wipe out "reivers," or outlaw clans such as the Armstrongs and Grahams. These clans were "broken" by James and stripped of their land and arms.

However, there was still the age-old threat from the Highlanders. In Scotland, the two groups, Highlander and Lowlander, continued to be contemptuous of each other. Each lived a life entirely foreign to the other.

Ulster

℃

across the Irish Sea, other events were transpiring. For five centuries, ever since Henry II invaded Ireland in the twelfth century, the English had tried to control the island. But the Irish people steadfastly resisted. By the time Queen Elizabeth took the crown in 1558, the Irish problem had become a financial drain on the English treasury. English control was reduced to a small area around Dublin called "The Pale." Everything "Beyond The Pale" was controlled by the war-like Irish Chieftains.

In 1595, the Earl of Tyrone led an alliance of Irish clans against the English. Elizabeth sent an army of 20,000 troops to crush them under the Earl of Essex. Essex failed and was called back to England in disgrace. Elizabeth then sent Lord Mountjoy to Ireland who began a campaign of destruction which pre-dated Sherman's march to the sea by 250 years. He destroyed crops, slaughtered cattle, and burned houses, as well as defeating Irish armies in the field. The Irish were starved out as well as beaten militarily. Northern Ireland was, for the most part, depopulated.

Elizabeth had earlier tried to establish English farmers in Northern Ireland but the effort had ultimately failed. The English settlers were too few to form effective military resistance against the native Irish. When Elizabeth died in 1603 and power passed to James I, he took up the issue. James understood the difficult conditions in Scotland and its proximity to Northern Ireland. He knew the Scots were tough, adventurous, and wouldn't turn down a bargain. Furthermore, unlike the Irish, they were loyal subjects. So he made the Scots an offer they couldn't refuse. Those who chose to migrate to Northern Ireland would receive a "feu" or lease for twenty-one years or even for life in almost virgin territory. In Scotland, leases were of much shorter duration and the soil was poorer.

So James, "'out of unspeikable love and tinder effection for his Scottish subjects,' had decided that they were to be allowed participation."[56] He opened Northern Ireland for settlement in 1610. In the same proclamation, he stated the obvious, that the Scots, "lye so neir to that coiste of Ulster that they could easily transport men and bestiall."[57] Large land grants were parceled out to English and Scottish lords called "undertakers." For each 2,000-acre parcel, a lord agreed to bring "forty eight able men of the age of 18 or upwards, being born in England and or the inward parts [Lowlands] of Scotland."[58] He was further instructed to "grant farms to his tenants in sizes specified; and, he must have a stock of muskets and hand weapons to arm him and his tenants."[59] Historian James Leyburn writes: "Galloway, that region of the Southwest which included the shires of Ayr, Dumfries, Renfrew, Dumbarton, and Lanarc, provided the greatest number for the obvious reason that it was closest to Ulster."[60]

There were already Scots in Northern Ireland. As early as the 1300s, they had come to Ireland as mercenary soldiers or "redshanks" to join the armies of Irish kings against the English. Robert Bell tells us "from the mid 14th century MacDougals or MacDowells are recorded as galloglasses [mercenaries] in Ireland, particularly in Rosecommon."[61]

It is possible that people already spelling their name "McDill" had come with their fellow MacDowall clansmen as galloglasses or mercenary soldiers. Unfortunately, a shortage of early Irish records prevents either proof or disproof of this. But since we know for certain that McDills had existed in Scotland as early as 1526, it is reasonable to assume that McDills, already bearing the name, migrated to Ireland after settlement was opened in 1610.

Ireland, twenty-five miles across the Irish Sea, must've looked much the same to those Scots in 1610 as it had to the Romans in 82 A.D. The green mountains rising in the mist and the sparkling shore and fertile valleys beckoned to them just out of reach. But unlike the Roman legions, who never set foot in Ireland, the Scots crossed the Irish Sea with everything they owned. They knew an opportunity when they saw one.

Among those immigrants who moved provisions, animals, and implements between 1610 and 1675 were surely families of McDills. In a letter from the Ulster Historical Foundation, the writer stated, "The Hearth Money Roll for County Antrim was compiled in 1669. There were three references for individuals named John McDill. The Hearth Money Roll was a tax on hearths and it is clear that there were McDills living in County Antrim in [as early as] 1669 . . ."[62]

Along with the Scots who migrated were Anglo-Celtic people from the Northern shires of England, the same "borderers" the border Scots had fought for centuries. Also many of the Scottish "reivers" or "riding clans" mentioned earlier were motivated to emigrate. Without lands and sometimes with prices on their heads, these "broken men" had no other place to go. They, along with others, would become members of a race of people later called Ulster Scots, Scots Irish, or Scotch Irish.

In spite of a thousand years of contact between Ulster and the Scottish Lowlands, in the form of conquest, settlement and trade, by 1610, the Lowland Scots were thoroughly Scottish. Furthermore, they were almost wholly Protestant. What they found in Northern Ireland was solidly entrenched Catholicism. The Jesuits had firmly reestablished the faith in Ireland while the Reformation swept Scotland. To be Irish was to be Catholic.

When the Scots moved into Northern Ireland, we see the beginning of the conflict of nationality and religion that still exists there today. The understandable hatred for the Scots who'd been given Irish land transformed Ulster into a war zone. In the rebellion of 1641, the Irish natives made their mightiest effort to drive out the Scots. The fighting lasted for eleven years. There were at least 15,000 casualties. Two-thirds of those probably died of privation. About one-seventh of the total population of colonists in Ulster died.

Covenanters

Soon another religious conflict would erupt. Earlier Henry VIII of England had broken with Rome and established the Church of England or Anglican Church. In the 1630s, King Charles I began attempting to bring Scottish Presbyterians under the Church's control. In defiance, a number of Scottish Presbyterians in Scotland and in Ulster formed a "covenant" with English Puritans, pledging to resist the crown's attempt to force a hierarchy of church officials on them. These Scots called themselves Covenanters. Charles I was concerned that the General Assembly of the Kirk (Scottish Church) might be, by its authority and independence, a threat to his power. He preferred England's version of the Reformation. In the Anglican Church, bishops and church officials answered to the King.

From their pulpits, Presbyterian ministers incited the people against Charles' authority. The Scots then saw venerated leaders of the Kirk arrested and led like criminals through the streets of Edinburgh. Leyburn states:

> There followed now in Scotland the "Killing Times," when the resolute and fierce Covenanters of the Western Lowlands [and Ulster] fought their guerrilla warfare against the King's men. Refusing to accept episcopacy and determined to worship God after their own fashion, they left the towns to hold their meetings on hillsides and in secluded valleys. They carried arms to defend themselves against the soldiers who were sent to hunt them down. Many were killed on the borders; hundreds were cast into prison, others were tortured, and some were hanged; but nothing could tame their spirit. If martyrs are the seed of the church, the Scottish Church now had its martyrs to increase its strength.[63]

More Troubles

§

At the same time, England became divided between two political factions, the Royalists (those loyal to King Charles I) and the Parliamentarians who wanted the King's power limited by Parliament. Eventually Parliament became dominated by Oliver Cromwell and the Puritans. Cromwell, who would later declare England a Protectorate and himself Lord Protector, took power. But when the Puritans beheaded Charles I in 1649 and ejected Presbyterians from the House of Commons, Scots changed sides. Ulstermen organized an armed rebellion. Their Irish Catholic neighbors also rebelled. Cromwell himself crossed to Ireland in 1650 and crushed Catholic and Presbyterian opposition alike, putting Ireland to fire and sword. Three-sevenths of the population, or 616,000 people, perished by war, famine, and plague. About 500,000 were Irish and 100,000 Ulster Scots. Ireland was subdued.

When Cromwell returned to England, war between the Ulster Scots and native Irish was resumed. Towns like Londonderry became fortresses. The siege of Derry in 1689 gave the Scotts a new phrase: "no surrender," one still used until recently. By most accounts, there was very little intermarriage between the two people. The intense dislike between the two groups kept them at arms length. The Irish hated the Scots and kept their women at home.

But amid all that adversity, the Scots thrived. Ulster, formerly a near wilderness, was transformed into the most prosperous part of Ireland. From the remaining English settlers, the Scots learned more advanced farming methods. They also learned to drain bogs and swamps and to plant the potato, which had recently been introduced from America by Sir Walter Raleigh. Bushmill's Distillery was established on the coast of County Antrim and a whiskey business started.

Sheep flourished in Ulster. The settlers made woolen cloth and took it to the seaport towns to market. They acquired a reputation for land bargaining, thrift, and even stinginess that persists to this day. A visiting Englishman once said they "keep the Sabbath and everything else they can get their hands on." They were also described as having "deep pockets and short arms." Scotland's thin soil, plagues, and insecurities had made them tough, frugal, and hard working. In Ulster they prospered.

The Ancestors and Descendants of Robert Nathaniel McDill

The Test Act

ℭ

In the 1700s, religious oppression returned. During the reign of Queen Anne, the Anglican High-Church dominated politics. In 1703, Queen Anne passed the Test Act. This law required that all office holders in Ireland take the sacrament according to the prescriptions of the Established Church (Church of England). What once pertained only to Catholics was now applied to Presbyterians as well. Substantial members of the Presbyterian Church who would ordinarily have been candidates for magistrate and other civil posts were no longer eligible. Catholics and dissenters (Presbyterians in both Scotland and Ulster) were not allowed to buy land or take out a lease for longer than thirty-one years. They were also barred from teaching school and not permitted to bury their dead unless an Episcopalian priest officiated at the funeral. It was announced that all children of Presbyterian marriages should be regarded as bastards.

But a new and rebellious mindset, nurtured by the Presbyterian Kirk, had evolved. Scotland had developed the Calvinistic doctrine that civil government, though necessary, was only legitimate when it was according to the will of God. This attitude toward the established Church of England would soon be applied to governments. James Webb writes:

> This meant not only that the Kirk would have the power to organize religious activity at the local level, but also that Scots had reserved the right to judge their central government according to the standards they themselves would set from below. This decision that the laity at the lower levels of society would directly participate in judging their higher-ups was a daring and astonishing concept for the times, even though it had emerged naturally from more than a thousand years of historical experience.[64]

The Clearances

੬

A series of famines occurred in the early 1700s. Events finally conspired to bring all of Ireland to its knees in 1741. Historian Jonathon Bardom relates:

> *[A] Shortage of seed and further bad weather led to a terrible famine in1741. In the wake of this famine, at its most severe in Ulster, fever exacted a fearful toll during the hot summer of 1741. The Irish called this blaidhain an 'air, year of the slaughter; perhaps around 300,000 died, a death toll in proportion as terrible as the Great Famine of the 1840s. The meager documentary record of this calamity is an indication that such acts of God were still considered a normal feature of the human condition in Northwestern Europe in the early 18th century. The people of Ulster who suffered most and who died first were the poorest of the Catholic Irish; but the English and Scottish settlers had come to the north of Ireland to find a better life and when the expectations of many had not been fulfilled they moved on across the Atlantic to the New World.[65]*

By the mid 1700s, long-term leases were being divided into smaller and smaller plots. Drought, smallpox, and a destructive sheep disease followed. Then, in 1770, leases on the huge estates of the Marquis of Donnegall expired. R. J. Dixon relates:

> *Donnegall, preferring cash in hand to an increase in annual income, wished to relet the estate at its former rent and raise 100,000 pounds in fines [payments] as compensation for this concession. This sum, which amounted to between*

The Ancestors and Descendants of Robert Nathaniel McDill

three and four times the annual rental of the estate, was far beyond the means of most tenants who found a single year's rent an ample burden. Outrages followed ... during the next year, the disturbances spread. Generally, under the name of "Hearts Of Steel," the malcontents maintained a lawless, turbulent and dangerous spirit of insurgency throughout 1771 and 1772, their activities ranging from attempts to regulate rents to the fighting of pitched battles against the troops sent against them.[66]

Other landlords were raising rents as well. And if that were not enough, in 1771 and 1772, foreign demand for Irish linens fell by almost half. After the murder of a minister who was trying to calm an angry crowd in 1772, troops arrived. Jonathon Bardon relates:

The Army arrived soon afterwards for this had been only one episode of a series of disturbances causing the Irish Parliament to rush through "An Act for the more effectual punishment of wicked disorderly persons in Antrim, Down, and Armagh, the city and County of Londonderry, and County Tyrone." As soldiers spread through the province they crushed the uncoordinated uprisings, men were tried and hanged, and it was reported that many insurgents were drowned while attempting to escape to Scotland in open boats. Lord Townsend, the Viceroy, ordered a general pardon in November 1772 and privately condemned the landlords whose rents "were stretched to the utmost."[67]

Rent increases coincided with a succession of harvest failures between 1770 and 1772. By 1773, bread prices were close to what they had been during the famine of 1741.

Lords were also raising rents dramatically back in Scotland. If tenants balked, they were simply evicted. There was more money to be had in raising sheep for the wool trade than in renting to farmers. This Highland version of the evictions became known as the "Highland Clearances." In 1773, Samuel Johnson and his biographer, James Boswell, made their famous tour of the Scottish Highlands. Johnson and Boswell watched ship after shipload of Scottish Presbyterians leaving the Highlands and Western Islands for the Colonies. Johnson remarked, "Those who left before…were generally the idle dependants of overburdened families, or men who had no property and therefore carried away only themselves."[68] But in 1773, he saw a different immigrant. "Those who were considered prosperous and wealthy sell their stock and carry away the money. In some parts there is now reason to fear, that none will stay but those who are too poor to remove themselves."

Northern Ireland was being drained as well, not only of its people but also of its money. Bardon writes:

> *When the economic crisis struck in 1770, immigration to America reached a new peak of about 10,000 a year. A very high proportion of those leaving were linen weavers, many of them tenant farmers who sold their interest in their holdings to have some capital to make a new start. In April 1773, the Londonderry Journal reported that one ship had no less than 4000 pounds sterling on board.[69]*

The Ancestors and Descendants of Robert Nathaniel McDill

America

$\mathscr{C}$

While Scots-Irish and Scots alike were being forced out of their homes, they were also being offered a new opportunity elsewhere. Across the Atlantic Ocean, a new land awaited, the American Colonies. The British Crown was intent on seeding its possessions in the New World with what it believed to be loyal subjects. Land was free to any colonist willing to take up plow and musket. For years, the Colonies, considered a backwater by most Englishmen, had been mostly left alone to pursue their own interests. This had resulted in unprecedented freedom. "Broadsides" or pamphlets were circulated in Britain and Ireland advertising the benefits of life in the New World. There were also letters written home by family members who had already immigrated. These mitigated many of the fears of prospective immigrants. Concerning those years following the violence of 1771 and 1772 in Ulster, James Leyburn states: "During the next three years nearly 800 vessels sailed from ports in the North of Ireland, carrying as many as 25,000 passengers, all Presbyterian."[70]

The economic condition of the immigrants from Northern Ireland has been a point of contention. Leyburn, quoting a writer of the time, claims that "the people of Ulster had, by 1770, become poor, living chiefly on potatoes and milk and oat bread. Their little farms had been divided and subdivided until the portions are so small they cannot live on them."[71] But R. J. Dixon states that "after 1771 those who immigrated were paying passengers of the middle-class laid low by a double blow, this class saved what it could from the ruins and invested part of the proceeds in the cost of a passage to the land of hope."[72] Some Ulster immigrants were less fortunate than either of these views might indicate. One Irish scholar states naval records revealed that, from 1745 to 1775, 5,835 Scotch-Irish came to America as indentured servants. But this is a tiny fraction considering the total number of immigrants. David H. Fischer tells us, "As always in a voluntary migration, desperately poor people were excluded by the fact of poverty itself. The cost of a family's passage to America was high enough to keep the poorest people at home."[73] No matter their economic condition, they all shared a common belief and a desire for a new beginning.

English historian J. A. Froude wrote:

> *Men of spirit and energy refused to remain in a country where they were held unfit to receive the rights of citizens. Religious bigotry, commercial jealousy, and modern landlordism had combined to do their worst against the Ulster settlement. Vexed with suits in ecclesiastical courts, forbidden to educate their children in their own faith, treated as dangerous in a state which, but for them, would have no existence and associated with Papists in an Act of Parliament which had deprived them of their civil rights, the most earnest of them at length abandoned the unthinkable service. They saw, at last, that the liberties for which their fathers had fought were not to be theirs in Ireland. During the first half of the 18th century counties Down, Antrim, Armagh and Derry were emptied of their Protestant families, who were of more value to Ireland than California gold mines.[74]*

These people, these Scots-Irish, had become a separate culture with its own mores and customs. Thousands of years of war and hardship had made them strong, independent, and wary. They were distrustful of governments and institutions because, in their experience, government and authority had too often represented usury and tyranny. They had little confidence in the law since laws had often been made to penalize them and favor those with more influence in Parliament. Magistrates and law officers had historically been tools of Princes and landlords. Therefore, they were reluctant to call on those in authority for help or protection. Everyman considered himself "sheriff of his own hearth."

Like their soon-to-be-planter neighbors in the Tidewater South, they were an "honor bound" culture. The security of self, property, and family depended on a man's reputation for being willing to fight to defend them. Defending one's "honor" could mean the use of fists or dueling pistols. Indeed, President Andrew Jackson, of Scots-Irish descent, participated in several duels.

Unlike their neighbors in New England, the descendents of Puritans and Quakers, who believed in "ordered liberty," i.e., liberty within the dictates of church and township, the Scots-Irish believed in "natural liberty," liberty granted by God. The Presbyterian Church had fostered in them a belief that they had the right to choose their own leaders and remove those who were not worthy. They would soon be part of a new nation that applied those principles to governments.

Two hundred thousand Scots had migrated to Northern Ireland and some two million of their descendants sailed for America in the 1700s. In 1776, it was estimated that one in seven American colonialists was Scots-Irish. Almost half of Ulster had crossed the Atlantic. Later, the emerging nation would need them badly. They would make up the vanguard of the westward movement, the pioneers who pushed America's borders into the wilderness of the Appalachians and beyond.

The Ancestors and Descendants of Robert Nathaniel McDill

Macdowall of Garthland

Macdowall of Freugh

Macdouall of Logan

Arms of the three main branches of the MacDowalls of Galloway.
Book plate provided by Leo B. McDowell.

The personal Coat of Arms of Fergus Day Hort Macdowell of
Garthland, Baron of Garochloyne, Garthland and Castle Semple,
chief of the Name and Arms of MacDowall. Used by permission.

A standard rendering of MacDowall arms. If this is hanging on your wall, no matter what variation of the name you bear, and you don't have specific permission to display it from the Lord Lyon of Edinburgh, I suggest you take it down.

The MacDowall shield or "plain arms," shared by all armorial branches of the MacDowall clan as well as the MacDougalls. "A fierce Lion royally crowned."

The MacDowall crest or badge. "Crests, which are the emblem on top of the helmets, encircled by a strap-and-buckle bearing the Chief's motto or slogan, may be worn as a badge by all of his name or clan."

The roofless ruins of Holyrood Abbey, burial place of Fergus MacDowall, first Lord of Galloway. He was born about 1078 and died 12 May 1161.

The ruins of Barr Castle, present seat of the MacDowall Clan.
All that remains is the central tower.

The Galloway countryside, a view toward the hills.

These ruins are believed to be on the site of St. Ninian's Chapel. St. Ninian, Scotland's first saint, established the first Christian church and school here at Whithorn in 397.

The Ancestors and Descendants of Robert Nathaniel McDill

Solway Firth on the South coast of Galloway.

The Rocky West Coast of Galloway, looking 25 miles across the Irish sea toward Ireland.

A Covenanter meeting in the mountains. Notice the man in the foreground with the musket, watching for the king's men.

The Ancestors and Descendants of Robert Nathaniel McDill

Part Two
The McDill Family Genealogy

"By today's standards, the journey was arduous."

John McDill
(~1675 – ~1761)

𝓮

According to one source, **John McDill** (Old John) was born in 1675 in Broughnow, near Broughshane, County Antrim, Northern Ireland.[1] He later married Janet Leslie who was also born in Ireland and bore him one daughter and six sons. He died in 1761 in Ireland.[2]

Broughnow no longer exists and there is no record of it ever existing. But early Irish records are scarce, and there may have once been a hamlet called Broughnow near Broughshane. John's parents' names are not known. John McDill was probably a farmer and surely a Presbyterian. It is almost certain that his progenitors migrated to Northern Ireland from southwestern Scotland, probably after the Ulster Plantation of 1610.

He was fourteen years old in 1689. Surely the big events of the day were talked about in his home. In that year, a Catholic force under the exiled Catholic King, James II of England, tried to replace the Protestant garrison at the walled city of Londonderry in Northern Ireland. The city resisted for 105 days until they were relieved by a Protestant army loyal to the new Protestant King William. It was estimated that 15,000 soldiers and civilians died of wounds, disease, and starvation. About the Siege of Derry, Jonathan Bardon relates: "For Protestants of Ulster this epic defense gave inspiration for more than three centuries to come."[3]

John saw the implementation of the Test Act in 1703. That act, during Queen Ann's reign, declared Presbyterians ineligible for civil posts, barred them from teaching school, and made it illegal for them to bury their dead without an Episcopal priest present. All Presbyterian marriages were deemed invalid and the children of those unions declared bastards. In Northern Ireland, Catholics and Presbyterians alike were not allowed to buy land or take out a lease longer than thirty years. This was sometimes circumvented, however, through clandestine dealings with

English neighbors.

Across the Irish Sea in 1707, the Scottish and English Parliaments passed the Act of Union which joined Scotland with England and Wales under one crown, that of Great Britain. John, who was thirty-two years old at the time, may have agreed with those who believed that Scotland had made a deal with the Devil. But the Act of Union turned out to be to Scotland's advantage. Scottish merchants and shippers were, for the first time, given freedom to trade with English colonies under the protection of the Royal Navy. Scottish merchants soon dominated the Virginia tobacco trade among other commerce. In less than one hundred years, Scotland was transformed into a prosperous nation.

John surely heard tales about the two Jacobite Rebellions back in Scotland. In 1715 and again in 1745, Jacobite armies made up mostly of Scottish Highlanders attempted to restore a Stuart (a descendent of the Bruces) to the British throne. The Rebellion of 1715 was crushed. After the Scottish defeat at Culloden in 1745, many Highland chiefs were executed. Highlanders were disarmed and the wearing of kilts and playing of bagpipes were outlawed. The restrictions weren't removed until 1782.

John also saw the first stages of the mass migration from Northern Ireland. Indeed he lived to see one of his sons, Hugh, leave Ireland for the American Colonies[4] before he died in 1761.[5]

The four children of John and Janet (Leslie) McDill that are known are:

- Margaret "Peggy" McDill, born August 1715 in Broughshane,[6] County Antrim, Ireland; died 1788 in Chester County, South Carolina; married in about 1730 to John Pedan born 1709, also in Broughshane, County Antrim, Ireland.[7]

- Thomas McDill, born about 1725 in Broughshane, County Antrim, Ireland; died 4 December 1794 in Chester County, South Carolina; married Margaret Chestnut, born 1 November 1739, died 6 December 1827 in Chester County, South Carolina.[8]

- Hugh McDill, born about 1738 in Ireland, died 1832 in Crawford County, Pennsylvania; married Roxanna Stuart.[9]

- **Nathaniel McDill**, born about 1740 near Broughshane, Racavan Parish, County Antrim, Ireland.[10]

Nathaniel McDill
(~1740 – ~1785)

𝒞

Nathaniel McDill was born about 1740 near Broughshane, Racavan Parish, County Antrim, Ireland.[11] He died some time before 16 April 1785, in Kershaw County, South Carolina.[12] While he was most probably the son of John McDill (Old John) and Janet (Leslie) McDill, his descent is not documented. In 1766, Nathaniel married Mary, whose surname is unknown.[13] Mary died after 1790, possibly in Chester County, South Carolina.[14]

Nathaniel's kinship to Thomas, Margaret, and John is established through a lifetime of associations. As tradition tells, John McDill (Old John) had one daughter and six sons.[15] One of John's sons, Thomas, and John's daughter, Margaret McDill Pedan, and their families accompanied Nathaniel and his family to the New World under the leadership of the same minister.[16] Another son, Hugh, settled in Crawford County, Pennsylvania.[17] Later, in South Carolina, Nathaniel would sell his original land grant and move his family, seemingly to be nearer his McDill and Pedan relatives. James Pedan, Nathaniel's probable nephew and Thomas's son, would one day be executor to Nathaniel's will. Thomas would be an overseer. Nathaniel remained close to his McDill and Pedan relatives all his life. All these links lead us to think that he was Thomas and Margaret's brother, and therefore John's son.

On the other hand, Mrs. C. Donnelly of the Ulster Historical Foundation reported that, according to the Connor Wills Index that covers County Antrim, there were two entries [at that period] for the name McDill.[18] One was for Nathaniel McDill of Racavan and the date of probate was 1761. The actual will was probably destroyed in the Dublin fire of 1922, as many others were. She speculated, rather wildly, that this may have been a relative of our Nathaniel McDill, possibly even his father.[19] However, she offered no proof. For our purposes, since Nathaniel is referenced as Thomas's brother in several genealogical texts (even though without documentation), and since so much evidence points in that direction, he will be considered so here.

Nathaniel was probably a farmer. He may have also worked in the linen trade. He was a Presbyterian and spoke with a broad Scots brogue. If he farmed land in Northern Ireland, it belonged to a landlord he had never seen, possibly the Marquis of Donegall.

By the mid 1770s, the Scottish Renaissance was in full bloom. Thinkers like the economist Adam Smith, the philosopher David Hume, and others had made the University of Edinburgh the most important seat of learning in the Western World. Historian Arthur Herman tells us: "By 1758, Horace Walpole, the son of a former prime minister [of England] had to admit 'Scotland is the most accomplished nation in Europe.' Voltaire agreed: 'It is to Scotland that we look to for our idea of civilization.'[20] The writings of those Scottish intellectuals were, at the time, being read and influencing the Americans who, in a few years, would become our Founding Fathers.

The Scottish Enlightenment was of little benefit to Ulster farmers, however. Religious persecution of Presbyterians had mostly dispelled by 1770. But Ulstermen were still being taxed to support the Church of England, the same Church of England that had long been a source of Scottish oppression. Times were hard for farmers. Furthermore, many Ulster Scots were employed in some facet of the textile industry, which was failing.

In 1770, when the Marquis of Donnegall drastically increased rents on his estates, anger rose to a breaking point. About that time, a "violent incident" occurred near Nathaniel's village. Legend has it that it involved an attack on one of Donegall's rent collectors. Some sources called it a murder. In the five years before 1770, only a handful of stories concerning disturbances caused by rents came out in Belfast's main newspaper. In the five years after, over ninety appeared.[21]

Into this volatile state of affairs stepped the Rev. Mr. William Martin, pastor of the Covenanter congregation at Kellswater. He stated in a sermon that he had received a "call" to go to South Carolina. In other words, he had been invited to pastor a new church in America. Furthermore, he would accept the offer. The group that contacted Martin was a small congregation of Covenanters in South Carolina. Historian Jean Stephenson writes:

> After some years the five or six Presbyterian groups, (Associate, Burgher, Anti- Burgher, Seceders, etc.) combined to build a union Church, which they called "Catholic," as all groups were to worship there. It was located on Rocky Mount Road, 15 miles southeast of Chester, South Carolina.[22]

The Rev. Mr. Martin then invited the congregation to accompany him. Jean Stephenson goes on to say:

> Presbyterian tradition is that he decided to go and, following an incident of violence resulting from higher rents, he preached a sermon calling on his congregation to accompany him. Whether this is true or not is immaterial, since the facts are clear that he did go and took with him a party of some 467 families and five ships.[23]

Indeed he did. The following advertisement appeared in the *Belfast Newsletter*:

> That as the Rev. Mr. William Martin of Kells-water, County of Antrim, having frequently heard of the Distress many are in for want of Gospel Ordinances dispensed to them in South Carolina, and being frequently urged and pressed by many of his Hearers and Acquaintances to go there, here at last firmly resolved (God willing) to be ready to embark at Belfast or Larne for thence, about the Beginning of September next: Therefore he thinks proper to give this public Notice to his present or former Hearers, or other well-disposed Families, that have a Design to embrace this favorable Opportunity to go to a Country where they may enjoy the Comforts of Life in Abundance, with the free exercise of their religious Sentiments. Dated Kells-water, December 25, 1771.[24]

Word soon spread about Rev. Mr. Martin's proposed immigration to South Carolina and members of other congregations and other sects joined the party. Nathaniel McDill was thirty-two years old at the time. He already had a wife and three small children.[25] The prospect of crossing a vast ocean with his young family to take up life in a colonial wilderness must have seemed daunting. But as we have seen, events seemed to leave him, and others like him, few other options.

At the same time that the Ulstermen were being forced out at home, they were being lured to the colonies. Ship owners encouraged immigration by circulating "broadsides" or pamphlets advertising opportunities in the New World. Friends and families, already in America, wrote letters home praising life there. There were McDills in Bucks County, Pennsylvania, as early as 1730.[26]

It was autumn. Nathaniel harvested and marketed his last crop. Everything was sold: animals, farm implements, furniture, and anything that could be converted into cash. Tearful goodbyes were spoken. Friends and neighbors knew that Nathaniel, Mary, and their three children would probably never return. They walked from their village to the port of Belfast, a distance of about thirty miles.

The five ships under the Rev. Mr. Martin's leadership were the *James and Mary*, the *Hopewell*, the *Lord Dunluce*, the *Free Mason*, and the *Pennsylvania Farmer*. Nathaniel and his family were berthed aboard the *Pennsylvania Farmer*.[27] On 22 December 1772, the following announcement was included in the shipping section of the *Belfast Newsletter*:

> Pennsylvania Farmer: *350 tons, Master C. Robinson; humanity and kind treatment greatly applauded. Agent: John Ewing, S. Brown merchants; Later added Rev. John Logue (Broughshane). Sailing postponed to allow farmers to dispose of their crops; Sailed from Belfast Oct. 16, 1772.*[28]

Another announcement boasted that the *Pennsylvania Farmer* "will be, single birthed, comfortable and would guarantee, agreeable passage."[29]

Aboard the *James and Mary*, another ship in the flotilla, were Thomas McDill, his wife, Mary Chestnut McDill, and their children. Also onboard were Thomas's sister, Margaret "Peggy" (McDill) Pedan, and her husband, John Pedan, who had been a Ruling Elder in his Church back in

Ulster,[30] and their children. Capt. John Workman commanded the *James and Mary*.[31] Thomas McDill and Peggy McDill were Nathaniel's siblings whom we mentioned earlier.[32]

All vessels that advertised passage to America boasted an abundance of provisions. But only a few gave details. One ship avowed, "beef and pork were among the provisions on board and that James Hunter, the master, was remarkable for his bountiful distribution of these."[33] Another, bound for Philadelphia, guaranteed each passenger "six pounds of good beef, six pounds of good ship's bread or six pounds of good oatmeal, as the passengers may choose to take; one pound of butter, or a pint of treacle or molasses and fourteen quarts of water per week."[34] This was probably unusually generous.

By today's standards, the journey was arduous. Living quarters were damp and fetid. Food and provisions sometimes rotted or proved insufficient. Days were long and tedious with nothing to interrupt the ship's roll or the endless horizons in all directions. There were horror tales of ships being becalmed (left adrift without wind) in mid-ocean and all aboard dying of thirst or starvation; or of pirates taking a ship by force and selling the passengers into slavery.

But Rev. Mr. Martin's group was blessed. All five ships made it to America. On 19 December 1772, the *Pennsylvania Farmer* docked in Charleston Harbor with Nathaniel and his family intact.[35] It had taken sixty-four days to cross the Atlantic. That was considered a good average crossing at the time, and it can be assumed that there were few mishaps.

The *James and Mary*, which sailed earlier, had docked on 18 October 1772, with Thomas McDill, Peggy (McDill) Pedan, and their families onboard. There had been tragedy onboard the *James and Mary*. But it appears Thomas and his fellow passengers considered themselves fortunate. Thomas was one of the signers of a letter that was later published back home in the *Belfast Newsletter* on 21 October 1772.[36] The letter informed all those at home that the *James and Mary* had arrived safely. The signers complemented the captain on the provisions and his treatment of the passengers. The signers also stated that: "we arrived here all well and in good spirits the 18th instant, [18th day of the month] (five children excepted who died in passage) after a pleasant and agreeable Passage of seven weeks and one day. Pleasant with respect to Weather and agreeable with regard to the Concord and Harmony that subsisted among us all."[37]

The deaths of five children being mentioned as a mere footnote indicates how tentative life was at the time. Thomas and his fellow passengers obviously considered the voyage a great success. The *James and Mary* was quarantined for a time in Charleston Harbor due to small pox.

Reverend Martin's Flotilla to Charleston:[38]

- *Pennsylvania Farmer* from Belfast: 64 days
- *Lord Dunluce* from Larne: 79 days
- *Hopewell* from Belfast: 64 days
- *Freemason* from Newry: 56 days
- *James and Mary* from Belfast: 54 days

Nathaniel's next act was to petition for land. His name appears on a document compiled in the Colonial Council Chamber on 6 January 1773.[39] The heading reads, "A list of passengers arrived in South Carolina from Ireland in the ship *Pennsylvania Farmer* and this day petitioned for land."[40]

Jean Stephenson states:

> *Persons who applied for land had to appear in person before the Governor in Council, and make their request, show they were of good character and in condition to improve the land by settling on it, etc. If the Governor was satisfied on these points and therefore decided the person was entitled to land, such fact was recorded in the Council Journal and the preparation of a warrant for survey was directed.[41]*

Nathaniel passed muster. The list of applicants was divided into two sections, those able to pay the various clerical and legal fees totaling five pounds and those not able to pay. A monetary bounty, given earlier by the English government to settlers, had, by then, been canceled. It appears that Nathaniel was able to pay the fees required. The fact that he had five pounds sterling in his purse in those harsh times leads me to think he was "close" with money. From my experience, that is a trait inherited by most of his descendants.

In January 1773, the Colonial Council granted Nathaniel 300 acres on Cedar Creek north of Broad River in Craven County.[42] As was the practice at the time, he received 100 acres for himself and an additional 50

The Ancestors and Descendants of Robert Nathaniel McDill

acres for each member of his household. Nathaniel's wife Mary and three children brought the total to 300 acres. The document reads:

> On 6 January 1773 South Carolina—Council met and N. McDill petitioned for Pursuant [sic] to a warrant from Jno. Brena Esq. D.L.G. dated the sixth day of January 1773, I have and laid out onto Nathaniel McDill a tract of land containing 300 acres, on the waters of Cedar Creek, north of Broad River, situated in Craven County, Bounded NW part on the Philip Showers land and a part on vacant land, and part on Shots land and SW part hath such shape and marks as the above plat represents.
> Signed: Feb. 15th 1773
> Jno. Alston D. L.[43]

Although Nathaniel's land was identified as being in Craven County, that county had been discontinued in the year 1769. It had been comprised of a huge portion of northern South Carolina with the Mississippi River as a western boundary. In 1769, the far western portion became Camden District. Still later in 1798, the counties of Chester, Kershaw, Fairfield, and Richland, among others, were created when Camden District ceased to exist. Cedar Creek, on the north side of Broad River, is now in northern Richland County. This is probably where his land was located.

In Charleston, Nathaniel bought farm implements as well as provisions to last the family through the first hard year. They may have carried their possessions on their backs. Or they may have purchased an ox and cart. If so, it's interesting to imagine the family's 150-mile trek inland. Nathaniel's oldest daughter was six at the time. Son James was four and another daughter was two. Nathaniel walked in front, leading the bullock. There was another child on the way.

The land they had been granted was part of a vast wilderness. But to Nathaniel and his contemporaries, it represented the realization of a dream. After a lifetime of toiling for absentee landlords and being subject to the whims of Kings and Parliament, this was something that would truly be his own. Instead of a tenant, he would become a landowner. And finally, he was free to enjoy the fruits of his own labor in peace and plenty.

When the family arrived at Cedar Creek, Nathaniel's first act was to fell enough trees to build a small log pen or cabin. It was a crude, four-sided affair with only a dirt floor. Perhaps his new neighbors helped him raise the walls. These pioneer cabins were usually improved and added on to later. As Nathaniel cut down trees to build his cabin and provide fuel, he was also clearing land. He probably cleared only a few acres, enough to grow the staples that his family needed. He didn't plant oats or flax as he might have done in Ulster, but what had been most successful for his neighbors. Historian, David H. Fischer relates:

> New American vegetables...appeared on backcountry tables. Most families kept a "truck-patch," in which they raised squashes, "cushaws" (a relative of squash), pumpkins, gourds, beans and sweet roasting ears of Indian corn. Many families also raised "sallet" greens, cress, poke and bear's lettuce...the ingredients were new, but the consumption of "sallet" and "greens" was much the same as in the old country.[44]

Potatoes were also an important garden crop.

Then Nathaniel set to work building up herds of hogs and cattle that he marked or branded to show ownership. His hogs ran loose in the woods fattening on mast such as beechnuts, acorns, and roots. He fenced in his crops and garden plot to keep out the free-roaming livestock, his own and his neighbors. Hogs and cattle were the major sources of income for Nathaniel and the other settlers in the area. By the Civil War, Southerners from the interior regions were driving over four million hogs a year to market, and probably as many cattle.

The traditions of open range and herding were definitely Celtic. Even though much of Ulster was fenced by 1772, Celtic immigrants to the colonies from Scotland, Ireland, and Wales quickly found that the wilderness they had inherited in the American South was perfectly suited for their ancient ways. And in the Southern states, these Celtic immigrants predominated. Warmer climates and plentiful grass and mast meant that cattle and hogs could be left outdoors unattended all year round. Historian Grady McWhiney states, "Celts had been open range pastoralists since antiquity, and they continued to be open range pastoralists in the American South."[45] In the meantime, colonists in New

England who were mostly English were building a country of small towns and fenced farms. There, crops were the main source of income. Animals were housed indoors and fed during the cold winters. "Good fences make good neighbors," said one of Robert Frost's Yankees.[46]

Concerning the backcountry pioneer diet, David Fischer tells us, "One important staple of this diet was clabber, a dish of sour milk, curds and whey which was eaten by youngsters and adults throughout the backcountry, as it had been in North Britain for many centuries."[47] But in other ways, the diet was adapted to the new environment. "Oats yielded to maze, which was pounded into cornmeal and cooked by boiling. But this was merely a change from oatmeal mush to cornmeal mush or "grits" as it was called in the southern highlands. The ingredients changed, but the texture of the dish remained the same."[48] Pork replaced the mutton that had been a meat staple in Scotland and Northern Ireland.

On 31 August 1773, Nathaniel posted a Memorial.[49] This was a legal declaration required by South Carolina law. Holders of royal grants were required to register their land so "quit rents" (a tax) could be collected for the crown. On 4 March 1775, Nathaniel appeared in court where he gave his oath in regard to a deed he had witnessed.[50] In 1778, Nathaniel was named on a list of Petit Jurors between Broad and Catawba Rivers.[51] This location is compatible with his land holdings on Cedar Creek in what later became Richland County.

Earlier, Nathaniel's brother, Thomas McDill, and wife Margaret Chestnut McDill, had settled on 400 acres in Craven County on a branch of Rocky Creek. They received the grant on 21 April 1774. Thomas's land adjoined, among others, the property of Margaret's father, David Chestnut.[52] The grant was located north and slightly east of Rocky Creek in what is today western Chester County. Thomas and his family were near their church and the Rev. William Martin.

John Pedan and Margaret McDill Pedan initially settled a little farther west. They received land in Craven County on "Ferguson Creek, waters of Tiger River," which was granted to John Pedan on 11 Dec 1772. Later, during the Revolution, they and some of their children relocated to the Rocky Creek area nearer family and church.[53]

As stated earlier, the Covenanters in the Rocky Creek area in the southeastern portion of Chester County had written home in 1770 asking for a minister. It was in response to this call that Rev. William Martin came to South Carolina as the first Covenanter minister in the South. Many of the party he brought with him were able to settle around Rocky Creek near their leader.[54] At first, Reverend Martin preached at the established Presbyterian Church called Catholic, meaning five or six Presbyterian groups, Associate, Covenanter, Burgher, Anti-Burgher, Seceders, etc. were all included. But, as Jean Stephenson tells us, "in 1774 the Covenanter congregation withdrew from Catholic and built a log church on the same road as the Catholic Church and two miles east of it, on the dividing ridge between Great and Little Rocky Creeks."[55]

Between 1778, when Nathaniel was listed as juror in Camden District, and 1783 when he wrote his will, he moved east to "Kershaw County," South Carolina, and took up land on Wateree Creek in the eastern portion of the county.[56] There, he was closer to his brother's family, his Pedan relatives, and his Church. Kershaw County was actually not yet formed, but many early deeds read that way. Anger had begun to foment among colonists against the British Crown as early as 1763. After defeating the French in the French and Indian war, the British Empire found itself in possession of all territory east of the Mississippi River except for New Orleans. The debt incurred from the war and the need to control this vast new region created problems.

King George III and Parliament decided to shoulder the colonists with a larger share of the burden of protecting British interests. A standing army was stationed in North America and colonists were ordered to provide living quarters and supplies for the troops. New taxes were levied on stamps, newspapers, legal documents, paint, molasses, and finally tea. Settlement west of the Appalachians was forbidden unless treaties with the Indians were established first. Old resentments were rekindled.

The British Crown had always treated American colonists as second-class citizens. Unlike the sugar planters in the West Indies, they were refused representation in Parliament. Tempers blazed and the British sent troops into Boston and New York. On 19 April 1775, a British force tried to seize the military supplies of the Massachusetts Militia. The people took up arms and turned them back first at Lexington and then at Concord. Word spread and the War for Independence was on.

Nathaniel McDill did not serve in the Revolutionary Army. However, his brother Thomas and nephews John and David did serve. Old records indicate that Thomas was in the battle of Wrights Bluff where his horse

The Ancestors and Descendants of Robert Nathaniel McDill

was killed.[57]

Thomas's son, John McDill, served from 1778 to 1782, both in the Regular Army and as a militiaman. He was in the attack on Congaree Fort.[58] It is interesting to hear part of his account of that campaign in his own words. In his pension application, as a veteran of the Revolutionary War, he stated the following account. He also lost a horse:

> *After the fall of Charleston, when the country was overrun by British troops and Tories, I joined General Sumter [Thomas Sumter] under the command of Captain Samuel Adams and Colonel Lacey [Edward Lacey], we marched to the Congaree Fort and besieged it for some time, was [sic] forced away and marched toward Charleston, on our route we met a party of British troops, attacked them—took and killed nearly the whole party and captured a number of wagons. Afterward we crossed the Santee River and attacked a troop of British soldiers—we were obliged to retreat having a number of our party killed and wounded and taken prisoners. I lost my horse, saddle and bridle.[59]*

Many colonists didn't participate in the conflict. During the Revolution, South Carolina saw its own civil war. Loyalties were equally split. Patriots and Tories (colonists loyal to the crown) burned and looted each other's farms and villages in a series of reprisals and counter reprisals. Many were murdered. A large number of pioneers simply chose to stay home and protect hearth and family. In Nathaniel's case, it's possible that his health was already failing. He would die in 1785 at the early age of forty-five.

After two failed attempts, the British finally captured Charleston in 1780. Then with the victory at Camden, the British and their Tory allies controlled most of South Carolina. But in October 1780, an event took place that turned the war in the colonists' favor. At the Battle of Kings Mountain in South Carolina, a large militia of Scots-Irish frontiersmen defeated an army of loyalists and British regulars commanded by the crack Scottish General Patrick Ferguson. In reprisal for past British atrocities, Ferguson's entire army was slaughtered. After the battle, the militia disbanded and returned to their farms. Historians would later describe the event as "a gathering of the clans." News of Ferguson's defeat shocked loyalists. Many were then afraid to side with the British.

The Southern colonists handed the British another defeat at Cowpens on 17 January 1781. Volunteers began to flock to the Patriot cause. Ferguson's superior, Cornwallis, was forced to abandon his plan to cut off the Southern colonies. Instead, he took his army to Yorktown. There he found himself squeezed between the French fleet and General Washington's Colonial Army. Cornwallis had no choice but to surrender. The Treaty of Paris in 1783 officially ended the war.

The American colonists, through determination, courage, and blood, had wrenched their independence from the most powerful empire on earth. They were now free to build their own nation. It would not be a direct democracy in the Greek tradition, because the Founding Fathers were wary of the whims of the populous. It would instead be a republic, a nation of laws. The ownership of property would be sacrosanct. Each man would be equal before the law. All males between the ages of eighteen and forty-five, who were not already in the military, were deemed part of the "militia," and were expected to take up arms against foreign invaders whenever their nation called. Freedom of the press, freedom of religion, freedom of assembly—these and others rights were defined as "natural rights," or rights granted by God. The Constitution and the Bill of Rights, which would later codify those rights, were not intended to bestow these liberties on the citizens by government, but to prevent an overreaching federal government from usurping them.

The formation of our government owes much to the thinkers of the Scottish Enlightenment. For example, at the College of William and Mary, Thomas Jefferson's favorite professor was a Scottish emigrant, William Small, who taught the young Jefferson the works of Adam Smith, David Hume, and others. But there were two more major influences on the Founding Fathers: Englishman John Locke and Frenchman Charles de Montesquieu. For millennia, theorists held the belief that the common man was incapable of governing himself. Plato, Thomas More, and Thomas Hobbes had constructed fantasy utopias where man's selfishness and aggression were to be held in check by philosopher kings or benevolent sovereigns. They also proposed doing away with private property to guarantee that no man possess more than another.

But Locke, who lived from 1632 to 1704, not only understood the true nature of man, he trusted him. According to Locke, in a just society,

The Ancestors and Descendants of Robert Nathaniel McDill

each man was his own ruler and was born with God-given inalienable rights. Locke believed in "natural law," the customs and behavior that evolve naturally among men so they can live together and conduct commerce.

Montesquieu understood history's preference for tyrants and explained that liberty must be guaranteed within the context of a constitution or fixed set of laws. These laws would control the governors and limit their powers. He outlined an ideal government with three separate branches. This "separation of powers" guarded against abuse. They would be the legislative, the judicial, and the executive branches. These ideas formed the basis of our Constitution.

But Nathaniel McDill didn't live to see the Constitution adopted. He wrote his will on 24 September 1783 and died by 16 April 1785 at the age of forty-five in Kershaw County, South Carolina, where the will was probated.[60] He left behind Mary and seven children. Nathaniel is buried in Kershaw County.

> *In the name of God Amen, I, Nathaniel McDill of Watery [sic] Creek, being weak in body but sound of memory, blessed be God for it, on the 24th day of September in the year of our Lord 1783, I do constitute, make and publish over this my last will and testament in manner and form as follows. I do give and request all my alliance, goods, and chattels, rights and privileges to my well beloved wife Mary and my seven children to be equally divided among them at the time they part, and I order them to live together until there be a lawful reason for them to part. I make an[d] ordain William Boyd and James Pedan [nephew, son of Thomas] my soul executors and I make Thomas McDill and James main [sic] overseers of this my will to take care and see the same performed according to my true intent and mining [sic]. I also empower these four men executors and overseers to sell or dispose of the plantation I now live on and to buy or purchase another where they think will answer my family best to live on. In illness, I, said Nathaniel McDill, do confirm this my last will and testament with my hand and seal, the day and year above written.*

Signed, Sealed, and delivered in the presence of
David Carnes
Hugh Smith
Natha. [sic] *McDill (seal)*
Not recorded, proved April 16, 1785

In 1790, the "Widow McDill" was living in Camden district, Chester County, South Carolina, near Thomas McDill and John McDill, Nathaniel's brother and nephew.[61] In her household, at the time, were two males and five females. Chester County was adjacent to Kershaw County in 1790. She may have been the female over forty-five years old in "Nat" McDill's (Nathaniel Jr.) household listed in the 1810 census of Fairfield County, South Carolina.[62]

Probable children of Nathaniel and Mary McDill:

- Female McDill, born about 1767 in Ireland.

- James McDill, born about 1769 in Ireland; died 12 June 1847 [or Sep. 1846] in Fairfield County, South Carolina; married Mary Boyd on 10 February 1803 in Fairfield County, South Carolina.

- Female McDill, born about 1771 in Ireland.

- Female McDill, born about 1773.

- **Nathaniel McDill, Jr.**, born 1775 in South Carolina; died 20 January 1857 in Tallapoosa County, Alabama; married in about 1814 to Ann.

- Sarah McDill, born about 1777 in South Carolina; died after 1830.

- Margaret McDill, born about 1783 in South Carolina; died October 1861 in Fairfield County, South Carolina.

Nathaniel McDill Jr.
(~1775 – ~1857)

$\mathscr{C}$

Nathaniel McDill Jr. was born in 1775 in South Carolina, three years after his family arrived in the colonies. He was the fifth child and second son of Nathaniel McDill, the immigrant, and his wife Mary.[63] He died in January 1857 in Tallapoosa County, Alabama.[64] In about 1814, Nathaniel Jr. married **Ann,** perhaps Leslie or Logan, in South Carolina.[65] She was born about 1795 in that state and was twenty years his junior.[66] She died by 24 May 1872, in Elmore County, Alabama.[67]

American independence had been won from the British, and in 1787, the new nation had a Constitution. By 1790, the United States of America was standing on its own two feet, though tentatively. It was time to count the citizens. So in that year, the first census was taken. Nathaniel Jr., fifteen years old at the time, was found living in the household of his mother, the "Widow McDill," in Chester County, South Carolina.[68] His father, Nathaniel, had died five years earlier. Other family members in the household included Nathaniel Jr.'s older brother James, age twenty-one, and four of their five sisters.[69]

The Treaty of Paris, negotiated with the British in 1783, gained the new nation territory from the Appalachian Mountains west to the Mississippi River. Then, in 1803, the Louisiana Purchase added an additional 827,987 square miles. In twenty years, the United States had quadrupled in size.

In 1809, when Nathaniel Junior was 34, James Madison succeeded Thomas Jefferson as president. Britain and France were at war at the time, and both sides were seizing American merchant ships to keep supplies out of the hands of the other. The British also *impressed* American seamen, forcing them to serve on British ships. Finally France agreed to stop the practice. But Britain refused. At the time, many Americans also believed that the British were encouraging Indians to attack American settlers. Americans, especially in the South and West, called for war. At Madison's urging, Congress declared war on 18 June 1812. In 1814, British troops actually captured Washington D.C. and burned the Capitol and several other buildings. But the British were finally turned back. The Treaty of Ghent, signed 24 December 1814, officially ended the war. Neither side won and little was gained. By then, Nathaniel McDill Jr. was thirty-nine years old.

It may have been our Nathaniel Jr. who was listed as head of the household in Richland County, South Carolina, in the 1810 census.[70] He was said to be sixteen to twenty-six years of age. But this is inaccurate based on his 1775 birth. He would have been thirty-five at the time. Living with him were five females ranging in age from under ten to over forty-five. These could have been his sisters and one was possibly his wife or mother.

By 1820, Nathaniel Jr. and Ann had moved to Abbeville County, South Carolina, in the far western end of the state.[71] They had two sons and two daughters, all less than ten years old. There would eventually be eleven children.

There is no record of Nathaniel Jr. ever owning slaves. But during his lifetime, the issue would smolder and finally reach a crisis. Shortly after his death, the nation would explode into war.

In 1820, Congress drafted the Missouri Compromise in an attempt to cool rising tempers between the leaders of slave states and free states. The controversy arose when, in 1818, Missouri applied for admission to the Union. Southerners wanted Missouri admitted as a slave state and Northerners wanted it admitted as a free state. In either case, the balance between free and slave states would be upset. Congress worked out a compromise: Missouri entered as a slave state and Massachusetts gave up its northern territory forming the free state of Maine. Also, the land west of Missouri, which would possibly make up future states, would be free. The balance was maintained for the time with twelve free and twelve slave states. But the disagreement was far from settled.

In the meantime, advances in technology and machinery allowed for improvements to daily life for the settlers. In 1834, when Nathaniel Jr. was fifty-nine years old, Cyrus McCormick, the son of a Virginia farmer, patented the McCormick reaper. This horse-drawn machine enabled farmers to harvest up to ten acres of grain in a day. In 1837, Samuel F. B. Morse demonstrated his newly invented telegraph.

Federal troops rounded up the last of the Cherokee Indians in

Georgia in 1838, and forced them to move to the Oklahoma Territory. This march to Oklahoma was later called the Trail of Tears. It was a dark chapter in American history, as were most of our encounters with the Native Americans. For white settlers in the Southern states, however, it opened up rich new lands to the west.

Nathaniel Jr. moved into Georgia in advance of the eviction of the Cherokees. By 26 December 1837, he had purchased land in Coweta County, Georgia, from William Dillard for $900.[72] The tract was described as being in the second district of Coweta County and known as Lot #37. Witnesses to the deed were Jesse Stephens and James McClure. In 1840, Nathaniel Jr. was named in the census of Coweta County, Georgia.[73] He was sixty-five years old at the time, with Ann and eight of their eleven children living at home. The youngest, Isabella, was seven years old.

Ten years later, in 1850, the family still resided in Coweta County. They owned real estate valued at $1,200.[74] Only three children were living at home by then: Nathaniel Logan McDill, aged twenty; Amanda McDill, aged nineteen; and Isabella J., aged seventeen. Also in their household was George Spruill. He was the brother of Millie Ann Spruill, the wife of Nathaniel Jr.'s second son William. His occupation was given as "cabinet maker."[75]

Farther west, in Alabama, settlement of Indian lands had been thwarted by several bloody massacres during the early 1800's. But by 1840, federal troops had virtually cleared the area of Indians.[76] Nathaniel Jr. and his family continued their westward migration. In preparation for the move, they sold 202.5 acres in Coweta County, Georgia, to Robert Moore on 14 October 1850.[77] Nathaniel was, by then, seventy-five years old. Whether he and Ann were motivated to buy new lands or were simply moving to be closer to their children is uncertain. But on 7 October 1851, he was in Coosa County, Alabama, where he purchased property from Walker Reynolds and Hannah, his wife, for $80.[78] The land was described as the North Half of Section 34, Township 21, Range 21, in the Montgomery Land District.[79] A section is 640 acres, so if he bought half a section, it was 320 acres.

Senator Henry Clay of Kentucky and other moderates succeeded in bringing about another compromise on the slavery issue in 1850. The agreement allowed California to enter the Union as a free state and the slave trade was abolished in Washington D.C. To please the South,

Congress created New Mexico and Utah Territories and ruled that when they became states, the citizens could decide whether or not to allow slavery. Strict measures were also adopted to aid in the capture of runaway slaves. Many thought that the compromise of 1850 was the final solution.

On 14 January 1852, Nathaniel bought several tracts in Tallapoosa County comprising 160 acres from Henry Stricklin and his wife Armon for $640. The land was located in Township 23 and Range 22.[80] William McDill and William Evers were witnesses to the deed.

Nathaniel Jr.'s landholdings in Tallapoosa County then comprised approximately 480 acres as listed below, which he owned until his death.[81]

- N 1/2 Section 34, Township 21, Range 21—320 acres

- NE ¼ SE ¼ Section 35 Township 23, Range 22—40 acres

- NW ¼ SE ¼ Section 35 Township 23, Range 22—40 acres

- SE ¼ SE ¼ Section 35 Township 23, Range 22—40 acres

- NW ¼ SW ¼ Section 36 Township 23, Range 22—40 acres

On 17 February 1854, Nathaniel Jr. was listed in the 1855 state census of Tallapoosa County.[82] Two males lived in the household, one under twenty-one and one over twenty-one. Nathaniel may have included his son, Thomas, in his family, since Thomas was still unmarried. But Thomas also appeared in the census as living alone in his own household.

A final compromise on the slavery issue was attempted in 1854. Congress was considering the creation of new territories in the area between Missouri and present-day Idaho. Abolitionists claimed the land was part of an area in which the Missouri Compromise had guaranteed slavery would be "forever prohibited." But on 25 May 1854, Congress passed the Kansas Nebraska Act changing the provision. Two new territories, Kansas and Nebraska, were created and the people of those territories were to decide whether or not to allow slavery. Antislavery advocates were incensed.

In 1855, Nathaniel and Ann's daughter, Amanda, married James W. Hughes in Tallapoosa County, Alabama.[83]

Nathaniel McDill Jr. died in 1857 in Tallapoosa County, Alabama, at the age of eighty-two.[84] In 1860, his widow, Ann McDill, resided in the household of her daughter Isabella and Isabella's husband, David Sargent, in Chambers County, Alabama.[85] The census of that year indicated that she was then sixty-five years old and owned personal property valued at $1,000 dollars. She probably died between 1860 and 1870 during the decade of the Civil War. Ann was certainly deceased by 24 May 1872, when $50 was paid to her son-in-law, J. B. Hubbard, for the burial expenses of "Ann McDill, wife of Nathaniel McDill, deceased in Elmore County, Alabama."[86]

In 1871, Nathaniel's estate was filed in Tallapoosa County, where a division of his real estate identified his children as well as four apparent grandchildren. These were Flora E. McDill, Georgia Ann[87] McDill, and John A. McDill who were the children of Nathaniel Logan McDill.[88] They were identified as minors residing in Abbeville District, South Carolina.[89] The fourth grandchild was Jeptha Sprewell.[90]

Children of Nathaniel McDill Jr and Ann McDill, all probably born in South Carolina:

- Male McDill, born about 1815; died young.

- William McDill, born about 1870; married on 19 December 1839 in Coweta County Georgia to Millie Ann Sprewell. The couple lived in Pickens County Alabama in 1850. Moved to Amar County Alabama in 1880.[91]

- Female McDill, born about 1818.[92]

- Sarah M. McDill, born about 1819; married 26 December 1839 in Coweta County, Georgia, to John B. Hubbard;[93] of Elmore County, Alabama, in 1871.[94]

- James McDill, born 10 December 1820; married Mary E. Dawson, of Coosa County, Alabama.[95]

- Elizabeth Ann McDill, born about 1826; married Jonathan Prichard and was widowed or divorced by 1871 in Hickman County, Tennesseee.[96]

- **Thomas Alexander McDill**, born 26 November 1826; died 23 September 1909 in Newton County, Mississippi;[97] married 15 December 1857 in Chambers County, Alabama, to Sarah Elizabeth Callaham.[98]

- Nathaniel Logan McDill, born about 1830 in South Carolina;[99] married about 1853 to Ellen. Children, Flora E. McDill, born 1854 Alabama; Georgianna McDill born 1856 in Alabama;[100] and John McDill born after 1860, probably in Alabama, who was living in 1871 in Abbeville District South Carolina. Died in Lynchburg Virginia 29 March 1863.[101]

- Amanda McDill, born about 1831;[102] married 11 March 1855, in Tallapoosa County, Alabama, to James W. Hughes;[103] probably widowed by 1871 and living in Tallapoosa County, Alabama.[104] Amanda's husband was almost certainly James Wesley Hughes, 47th Alabama Infantry, 47th Regiment, Company F, who died 12/29/62 in Richmond City, Virginia at General Hospital # 22 from wounds received at the Battle of Fredericksburg. He is buried at Hollywood Cemetery, Richmond city, Virginia.[105]

- Isabella Jane McDill, born about 1833; married 1850–1860, to David Sargent;[106] of Chambers County, Alabama, in 1871.[107]

Thomas Alexander McDill
(~1826 – ~1909)

ℰ

Thomas Alexander McDill was born 26 November 1826,[108] in South Carolina. He was the eighth child of Nathaniel and Ann McDill.[109] Thomas died 23 September 1909 in Newton County, Mississippi.[110] He married **Sarah Elizabeth Callahan**[111] on 15 December 1857, in Chambers County, Alabama.[112] Sarah was born 14 July 1837[113] in South Carolina, the daughter of Samuel W. and Caroline Callaham.[114] She died on 25 September 1933 in Newton County, Mississippi.[115]

Thomas was born into a rapidly changing world. The nation was growing and eager settlers were following its new borders. Historians would later refer to it as the Era of Expansion. By the 1830s, pioneers had pushed the frontier beyond the Mississippi River, into Iowa, Missouri, Arkansas, and eastern Texas. The land beyond was called the Great Plains and was considered a worthless waste.

In 1836, Texans staged a successful revolt against Mexican rule. Nine years later, Texas joined the Union, giving the new nation vast lands beyond the Mississippi. In 1846, Britain ceded the Oregon territory to the United States, settling an old boundary dispute. In that same year, the U.S. easily defeated its weaker neighbor to the south in the Mexican war. The Treaty of Guadalupe Hidalgo, signed in 1848, gave the United States an area reaching all the way to the Pacific. Manifest destiny had become reality. The United States of America now spanned the continent. Between 1820 and 1849, the population more than doubled, reaching 22,488,000.

In the South, farmers raised cotton to supply the insatiable markets in England and the Northeast. The cotton gin had come into widespread use in the 1800s, providing a tremendous boon to cotton growers. With this invention, one man could separate as much cotton fiber from its seed in one day as fifty people had been able to do previously. New lands, suitable for cotton, had continued to open up in the South. As the Indians were forced out of Alabama and Georgia, settlers quickly moved in.

In 1840, young Thomas, thirteen years old at the time, was a member of the household of his father Nathaniel Jr. and mother Ann, along with his two brothers and five sisters.[116] They resided in Coweta County, Georgia. By 1850, at age twenty-three, Thomas had moved into the household of his older brother, James, in Abbeville County, South Carolina.[117] James and his wife Mary, possibly Boyd, had returned to South Carolina sometime earlier. James was not listed in the census as a landowner, but it may be that family members still owned land in the area and James had returned to farm it. Several McDill relatives lived nearby. Thomas listed his occupation as "cropper," which meant he was farming land on shares for his brother or someone else.

On 22 December 1852, Thomas McDill and David Sargent, his brother in law, purchased a parcel of land in Tallapoosa County, Alabama, from Archibald Meeks, his wife Phoebe, and Eligah [sic] Meeks, his son, for $300.[118] Thomas's older brother, William, was witness to the transaction. "Nat" McDill also signed as a witness. This was either Thomas' father or brother, Nathaniel Logan McDill. The land was described as the West half of the Northeast Quarter of Section 35 in Township 23, Range 22.[119] It contained eighty acres and adjoined the lands of his father, Nathaniel, on the north in Tallapoosa County.

The state census of 1855 listed Thomas, living alone in Tallapoosa County in the same area as his brothers, Nathaniel L. and William.[120] Another brother, James, also lived in the county.[121] Their father, Nathaniel, Jr., appeared in the census with two sons still at home, one over twenty-one and one under twenty-one.[122]

On 14 February 1857, Thomas McDill and his brother, James, jointly purchased eighty acres in Tallapoosa County from Jesse Nobles and his wife, Nancy, for $425.[123] The land was described as the Southwest Quarter of the Southwest Quarter in Section 25 and the Northeast Quarter of the Northeast Quarter of Section 35, both in Township 23, Range 22. This property was purchased in 1857, but the deed was not recorded in Tallapoosa County until many years later in 1890. Although the two tracts were in different sections, they touched each other at one corner.

On 1 March 1858, Thomas was granted eighty acres in Tallapoosa County by the U.S. government.[124] The land was identified as the "South Half of the Southeast Quarter in Section 26, Township 23, Range 22," placing it in central Tallapoosa County. It was adjacent and to the North of one of the above tracts and directly West of the other tract. This gave Thomas a total of 160 acres, although eighty of it was shared with his brother.

Thomas had recently begun a family of his own. On 15 December 1857, he wed Sarah Elizabeth Callahan in Chambers County, Alabama.[125] They were married by Thomas J. Williamson (probably either a minister or justice of the peace). The ceremony took place in the home of Sarah's father, S. W. Callaham, with M.L.D. Pittman as the second bondsman.[126] Chambers County is adjacent to Tallapoosa County where the couple made their new home.

Sarah was born 14 July 1837, in Alabama, the daughter of Samuel W. and Caroline Callaham.[127] For whatever reason, her name would appear throughout her life in documents as "Callahan." She was short in stature and her grandchildren would one day give her the nickname "Grandma Duck."

On 26 January 1860, Thomas McDill executed a trust deed in Tallapoosa County, Alabama, to his brother-in-law David Sergeant.[128] Two parcels of land were involved in this deed and the second tract of eighty acres was the 1858 grant. The document explains that Sargent was to use the value of the land to pay off three promissory notes to B. B. Patrick totaling $142 and three notes payable to John Brittace amounting to $112. If Thomas failed to pay the debts at maturity, then his brother-in-law was to sell the property and satisfy the debts. All the notes were due on 25 December 1860. Justice of the peace M. S. Strickland executed the paper and witnessed its signing. It was filed and recorded at Tallapoosa County on 3 March 1860.

On that same day, Thomas McDill executed a similar trust deed to U. E. Davis for eighty acres in two different tracks, "the Southwest Quarter of the South Quarter[129] of Section 25 of Township 23, Range 22 and the Northeast Quarter of Northeast Quarter of Section 35 in Township 23 of Range 22."[130] This was the land he had purchased with his brother James in 1857.

It is important to note that the two documents did not convey ownership of the land; they mortgaged it. While one might suppose that Thomas failed to pay his debts and that the land was later sold on the courthouse square, such was not the case as will be seen many years later.

In the spring of 1860, the McDills began another move. According to family legend, they had planned to go farther west than where events finally took them, possibly Louisiana, Texas, or even deeper into the frontier. Instead, their wagon broken down in Hickory, Mississippi. Another account has it that a member of the family became ill in Hickory, just before they were to embark with a large wagon train headed west.

It must be noted that Sarah's parents were already living in Newton County.[131] However, this neither contradicts nor corroborates family legend. In any event, the family settled in Newton County, 200 miles west of their previous home. Even then, it could not have been an easy journey. Like other pioneers of the time, Thomas and Sarah probably walked most of the way. Wagon space was needed for provisions, tools, and furniture. Daughter Sarah Elizabeth was not yet two years old and Sarah was pregnant with her second child. In these modern times, we look back on those years and wonder why families didn't simply wait until there was no babe in arms or no pregnancy before making the journey west. The truth is there hardly was such a time. Sarah Callahan McDill would eventually give birth to ten children.

The 1860 census of Hickory post office in Newton County, Mississippi, found them living next door to Sarah's parents on the border of Newton and Scott Counties.[132] Their son, John William, was probably not yet born as he was not included in the census.

It is not known whether or not Thomas was practicing the blacksmithing trade at that time. He was not a slaveholder, but he was no doubt a cotton grower as almost all Southerners were. Only about fifteen percent of Southern farmers owned slaves. The vast majority of slaves were owned by about five percent of Southerners.

But larger events were taking place beyond Thomas's control. Northeastern abolitionists had loudly condemned slavery. These descendants of Quakers and Puritans believed it to be morally corrupt as well as a violation of the very tenants on which the nation was founded. The massive slave trade of a century earlier, that had made many New England families rich, had now been forgotten. From early New England on, even into the 1800s, millions of black Africans were taken from the West Coast of Africa by New England and European sea captains and financiers and transported to the West Indies. That journey from Africa to the West

The Ancestors and Descendants of Robert Nathaniel McDill

Indies was called the "Middle Passage." Once there, the slaves were traded for sugar and molasses, which were taken back to ports in New England and distilled into rum. The rum was shipped back to Africa and traded for more slaves. Only five percent of those slaves reached the American South. Ninety-five percent were sold to sugar planters and other interests in the islands, Brazil and Central America. There had been voices against slavery in the South since the Revolution. Now those voices were bullied and threatened into silence by the powerful planters and cotton interests. So the South took a stand in defense of that abominable institution. But it would be a mistake to think that the average Confederate soldier fought to defend slavery. To believe that 95 percent of Southern whites were willing to fight and die to defend the rights of the remaining 5% who owned the majority of the slaves is ludicrous. They fought for what they believed to be their liberties and against what they feared was an overreaching and oppressive federal government.

From the Northern perspective, there was also the question of manifest destiny. The nation's empire, stretching from ocean to ocean, would be lost if the South were allowed to break away. Northern business interests also knew the cotton of the South was vital to Northeastern shipping and banking. If the Confederacy were allowed to ship its own cotton to Europe through New Orleans, Northeastern ports would be left high and dry. Neither the North nor the South would give in or compromise. The Southern States seceded from the Union.

Thomas was conscripted into the Confederate Army and mustered in at Enterprise, Clarke County, Mississippi, on 2 December 1862.[133] He was put in Company I, 36th Regiment of the Army of Tennessee, or Stevens Guards. The 36th was organized at Hickory Station, Mississippi, on 24 February 1862, under Captain R. D. Ogletree.[134] On his enlistment form, he gave his home as Newton County, Mississippi. However, years later, on 4 April 1930, when Sarah applied for a pension, as the widow of a Civil War soldier, she stated that she had lived in Mississippi sixty-two years.[135] That would place the date of their arrival in Mississippi much later, in 1868. But she was ninety-two years old at the time and her memory may have been fuzzy. May we all inherit her genes.

Like many others, Thomas was "conscripted," or drafted. It is not known whether or not he was a believer in the Southern cause. But for whatever reason, he did not volunteer. His age and family responsibilities may have been considerations. Sarah's first child, a daughter, Sarah Elizabeth, died young, but their second child, John William, was two years old at the time.[136] Thomas's Confederate service record describes him as having dark eyes, dark hair, fair complexion, and being 5' 9" in height.[137] He gave his occupation as wheelwright or blacksmith.[138]

Family tradition has it that Thomas served as a blacksmith during the Civil War because he was a small man. However, at 5' 9", he would have been considered better than average height in the mid-1800s. Indeed, Robert E. Lee was 5' 9" and considered tall. Generations later, McDills would look at pictures of Thomas as a very old man, shrunken and enfeebled, and conclude that he was small.

According to Confederate muster rolls and pay records, he apparently spent the balance of the war at Enterprise.[139] He may have been blacksmithing, repairing wagons and gun carriages. He may also have been a camp guard, since after 1863, he appears on the roster of Company A, Camp Guard. Some oral history has been handed down, however, concerning Thomas's war years. His grandson, Guy V. McDill, told later generations that Thomas claimed that he and his fellows, "spent most of their time running and hiding in the woods, trying to keep horses, wagons, and munitions out of the hands of the Yankees."[140] This quote obviously came to Guy secondhand since Thomas died before Guy's birth, but it certainly has the ring of truth. Indeed, Union forces were all over Mississippi during those years in their protracted effort to capture Vicksburg. Vicksburg finally fell on 4 July 1863.

While Thomas was at Enterprise, his regiment, the 36th, was part of the Army of Tennessee under the command of Gen. John Bell Hood. By 1864, the war in the West was going badly and General Hood decided that a bold stroke was necessary. He planned to recapture the city of Nashville. If successful, he might draw federal troops west and give Robert E. Lee's army breathing room back east. Nashville, the first Southern city occupied by the Union, had become a Union railhead and contained vast stores of munitions. By the time Hood marched his force up from the South toward his objective, the Army of Tennessee was a mere ghost of what it had been. On his way to Nashville, Hood blundered badly in an attempt to capture a large Union force under General John Schofield at Franklin. Against the advice of his subordinates, he ordered a frontal assault on the Union entrenchments. Six thousand, two hundred Confederates were

The Ancestors and Descendants of Robert Nathaniel McDill

killed or wounded.[141] After the battle, Schofield slipped his entire force through Hood's lines under the cover of darkness. The slaughter had gained Hood nothing.

The Army of Tennessee moved on to Nashville, however, and fortified a line south of the city. Under Union occupation, Nashville was a military stronghold manned by 250,000 well-armed and well-fed troops under U.S. General Thomas. Still, the Army of Tennessee, poorly provisioned and out numbered, moved in to lay siege. By December 8, they held a line south of Nashville five miles long. On December 15, Union forces attacked and forced Hood to take up a line several miles farther south. On December 16, Union General Thomas sent more troops against the left end of the Confederate line at Shy's Hill than Hood had in his whole army. The Army of Tennessee was smashed. What was left limped back to Mississippi.[142] After Nashville, the War in the West was all but over. Soon the official end came for the entire Confederate effort. Lee surrendered to Grant at Appomattox Courthouse on 9 April 1865.

Thomas's brother, Nathaniel Logan McDill, served in Company G, Sixth Alabama Infantry. The company was ordered to Virginia and Nathaniel Logan fought in the battles of Antietam, Fredericksburg, and the Battle of Seven Days. He was hospitalized in 1862 with "Catarrh" (cough) and Rheumatism. He fell ill again in March 1863, and died 29 March 1863, in General Hospital in Lynchburg, Virginia. Nathaniel Logan is buried in the Confederate section of the Old City Cemetery at Lynchburg.[143]

Thomas, then thirty-eight years old, returned to Newton County, Mississippi, where he and his family were to endure the hardships of reconstruction. On 10 January 1867, Thomas used his brother, James McDill, as an agent to sell his remaining lands in Tallapoosa County, Alabama.[144] The lands were sold to Rachel E. Conger for $800. There were four tracts totaling 160 acres. Two of the tracts were those purchased in 1857 from the Nobles. Interestingly, the deed of purchase for the land from the Nobles and the deed for the sale of the land to Rachel Conger were both recorded at the same time in Tallapoosa County in 1890, over thirty years later.

The 1870 census indicates that Thomas and Sarah were living in Newton County, Mississippi.[145] They owned personal property valued at $360. While they surely had money from the sale of the lands in Alabama, the census indicated that they owned no land. Four children lived with them, including two-year-old Robert Nathaniel. By 1883, Thomas had acquired 160 acres in "Section 6 of Township 7, Range 10, the East Half of the Northwest Quarter and the West Half of the Northeast Quarter."[146]

In 1900, Thomas and Sarah still lived in Newton County with four of their younger children.[147] His date of birth in the census was listed as November 1826 and Sarah's as July 1837. In this census, they indicate that they were the owners of a farm with no mortgage. They lived just a few households from Sarah's widowed mother, Caroline Callaham.

Thomas died 23 September 1909, in Newton County, Mississippi,[148] at the age of eighty-two. In 1910, the widow Sarah was the head of the household in Newton County and the owner of the family farm.[149] Sarah stated that she had borne ten children and that nine were still living. Their son Samuel and his wife Mattie lived with her.

Sarah outlived Thomas by twenty-four years, dying at the age of ninety-six on 25 September 1933, in Newton County, Mississippi.[150] In her old age, she suffered from cancer of the nose. Lindon Brown, a great grandson, stated in his memoir that July 14, Sarah's birthday, was a great holiday for the McDill family. Remembering a gathering he attended as a small boy, he wrote:

> *The celebration was held at the home of uncle Ed and Aunt Brucie McDill...There were aunts and uncles galore and cousins by the dozens. There was this long-long* [sic] *table under this huge oak tree.* [sic] *And enough food to feed a regiment. Uncle Ed had a large barn and on these days it was like a livery stable. I never remember seeing Great Grandpa. I think he had already died. But I do remember seeing Great Grandma. On that day children and I guess older people were [led] in quietly. She was on the bed covered with a white sheet. Part of her face was covered. [Cancer] had taken its toll. Still she was glad to see us.*[151]

Thomas and Sarah are buried in the Methodist Church Cemetery in Connehatta, Mississippi.

The Ancestors and Descendants of Robert Nathaniel McDill

Children of Thomas Alexander and Sarah Elizabeth (Callahan) McDill:

- Sarah Elizabeth McDill, born 10 September/November 1858; died 1859 in Alabama.

- John William McDill, born 22 May 1860 in Newton County, Mississippi; died 21 May 1920, in Newton County, Mississippi; married Mollie Dear.[152]

- Thomas James McDill, born 26 March 1863, in Hickory, Newton County, Mississippi;[153] married Annie Idelia Edwards.

- Margaret Nazarene McDill, born 20 June 1865;[154] married on 27 December 1888 in Newton County, Mississippi, to Joshua E. Bishop.[155]

- **Robert Nathaniel "Rob" McDill**, born 8 August 1867,[156] in Newton County, Mississippi; died 25 August 1960 in Union, Newton County, Mississippi; married 18 January 1898 in Scott County, Mississippi to Lida Adella "Dell" Cloud.[157]

- Mary Jane McDill, born 6 June 1870;[158] died 19 June 1928; married William Wesley Burns.

- Joseph Alexander McDill is buried in Fairhaven Memorial Park Cemetery, Santa Ana California. He had been living with his son Owen and daughter-in-law, Thelma Horton McDill. Joseph's Wife, Allie Estelle Hunt McDill died much earlier and is buried at Piketon Cemetery, Scott County, Mississippi. Daughters Mary Obera McDill Mitchell and Sybil Estelle McDill Laird are also buried at Piketon Cemetery. Annie Ruth McDill Richardson is buried at San Jacinto Valley Cemetery, San Jacinto California. Howard McDill is buried at Antioch Cemetery near Forest, Mississippi. Audrey Eugenia Gray is buried in Philadelphia, Mississippi. Earnest McDill is buried at Ellisville, Mississippi.[159]

- Samuel Morris McDill, born 7 May 1876;[160] married Martha

"Mattie" Anderson.[161]

ﻌ Ada Eugenia McDill, born 7 April 1878;[162] died about 1918; married on 29 November 1903 in Newton Co., Mississippi, to Dr. William C. Anderson.[163]

ﻌ Edward Wilder McDill, born 28 February 1881,[164] in Connehatta, Mississippi; married Alpha Brucie Pace.

Robert Nathaniel "Rob" McDill
(~1867 – ~1960)

𝒞

Robert Nathaniel "Rob" McDill was born 8 August 1867, in Scott County, Mississippi. He was the son of Thomas Alexander and Sarah Elizabeth Callahan (or Callaham) McDill.[165] He died 25 August 1960 in Union, Newton County, Mississippi.[166] Rob married for the first time on 18 January 1898, in Scott County, Mississippi to **Lida Adella "Dell" Cloud**.[167] She was born 24 June 1877, in Scott County, Mississippi, the second of three daughters born to Marquis Lafayette and Henrietta Virginia (Petty) Cloud.[168] Dell died on 19 June 1928, in Scott County, Mississippi.[169] On 27 June 1931, in Newton County, Mississippi, Rob married **Hattie Wall**. Hattie was born 1 October 1882 and died 22 July 1962.[170]

Rob came into the world not long after the close of the Civil War. At the time of the 1870 census, he was three years old and living with his parents in Newton County, the youngest of four children in the household.[171] When he was a boy, his grandfather Callaham, who was blind, took him on his knee, felt his bones, and announced to the boy's father, Thomas, that he would someday be a big man. Indeed, Rob grew up to be a large man and unusually strong.[172]

During most of Rob's life, the effects of the Civil War were apparent. The South had been laid so low that it didn't begin to catch up to the rest of the nation until the mid-twentieth century. One observer of the period put it this way: "No Army, no people were ever so thoroughly defeated." As a youth working on the family farm, Rob saw his family struggle against the boll weevil, unstable cotton markets, and a scarcity of money. He witnessed the era of Reconstruction and of Southern resentment. Indeed, his mother Sarah remained bitter toward the Union and the Union Army all her life. In Mississippi, there were lynchings and violence at the hands of the Ku Klux Klan to prevent former slaves from voting.

In 1876, when Rob was nine years old, Alexander Graham Bell made the first call on his newly invented telephone. In 1879, Thomas Edison invented the electric light.

Rob married Lida Adella "Dell" Cloud on 18 January 1898. She was the daughter of Marquis Lafayette and Henrietta Virginia Cloud.[173] Dell had blue eyes, dark hair, and light complexion. The 1900 census found them living in Scott County with their ten-month-old son, Robert Clinton, just a few households from Dell's parents.[174] Rob gave his occupation as farmer and the two owned a mortgaged farm. By 1910, they had purchased land in Newton County.[175] Three children lived with them at the time, and they owned the new farm free and clear.

In 1903, the Wright brothers made their first successful flight at Kitty Hawk, North Carolina. Later, Rob took his young family to an "air show" where they watched a "dare devil" take off from a cow pasture in a "flying machine." In 1927, when Rob was 60, Charles Lindbergh made the first solo flight across the Atlantic Ocean.

When Dell died in 1928, at the age of fifty from complications after undergoing gall bladder surgery, Rob became cautious of surgery of any kind.[176] He later warned his daughters-in-law against it.

On October 6, 1929, the New York Stock Exchange began its long decline. Billions of dollars of wealth were erased. The Great Depression had begun. Cotton farmers in the South had hardly recovered from the boll weevil scourge when they were laid low again by a worldwide economic slump. Rob saw many of those around him, black and white, reduced to desperation. But he endured. He held onto his farm when others were losing theirs. The Depression didn't end until well into World War II. In 1930, Rob was listed in the census as a widower living on the farm in Newton County, Mississippi.[177] His only daughter and three youngest sons lived with him. Several other McDills lived close by. At times, as many as three black families lived and worked on the farm.

Rob saw the horse and buggy yield to the automobile and bought a Model T Ford before the dirt roads of his rural county were paved. From the Sears and Roebuck Catalog, he ordered a battery-powered radio, which required a tall outdoor antenna. On Saturday nights, he and his family listened to the Grand Ole Opry from Nashville, Tennessee. His favorite performer was D. Ford Bailey, the little black harmonica player

The Ancestors and Descendants of Robert Nathaniel McDill

who performed "The Fox Chase," and "Dixie Flyer Blues."

On 27 June 1931, Rob married Hattie Wall in Newton County, Mississippi.[178] Hattie was born 1 October 1882, the daughter of Zachariah and Frances "Fanny" Wall.[179] During Dell's illness, Hattie had worked as Rob's housekeeper. At the time, it was perceived as a "marriage of convenience," but it grew into what appeared to be a loving relationship that lasted until Rob's death. Hattie was known to most of Rob's children and grandchildren as "Miss Hattie."

Rob offered all four of his sons land in exchange for a promise to stay in Mississippi and farm. To his disappointment, none took the offer. All four moved west to Texas and went into business.

Later in life, Rob saw mule teams replaced by tractors. Mechanized farm machinery reduced the need for human labor as well. Field hands and sharecroppers, with little work left for them, took their families and moved north to work in the new factories and mills of the Midwest.

He witnessed the coming of electricity and with it, inventions unheard of a few years before. Soon telephone wires linked Mississippi to the entire world. Finally Rob saw the introduction of air conditioning and television. On 4 October 1957, the Soviet Union launched Sputnik, the first space satellite, exacerbating the Cold War and setting off the Space Race.

When he was an old man and partially blind, Rob often took his *own* grandsons on his lap, just as his Grandfather Callaham before him had done. He felt their arms and legs and told their dads, "I believe he's going to be a big man." He died 25 August 1960 in Union, Newton County, Mississippi, while he and Hattie were living in the household of Rob's daughter, Onieda May, and her husband Walter Herrington.[180] Rob and Dell McDill are buried in the Sulfur Springs Baptist Church cemetery in Sulfur Springs, Mississippi. Hattie died on 22 July 1962 and is buried in the same cemetary.[181]

Children of Robert Nathaniel "Rob" and Lida Adella "Dell" (Cloud) McDill, all born in Newton County, Mississippi:

- Robert Clinton McDill, born 7 June 1899;[182] died 14 August 1939 in Beaumont, Jefferson County, Texas, of a coronary occlusion with chronic nephritis;[183] married Ann Gallet.

   Onieda May McDill, born 18 September 1906;[184] died 13 February 1999 in Newton County, Mississippi;[185] married on 27 April 1930 in Newton County, to Walter Herrington.[186]

   Marcus Alfred McDill (twin), born 26 April 1909;[187] died 17 May 1911 in Newton County, Mississippi.

   Male McDill (twin), born 26 April 1909; died 26 April 1909 in Newton County, Mississippi.

   Guy Vernon McDill, born 7 May 1910;[188] died 18 December 1973 in Beaumont, Jefferson County, Texas, of lung cancer; buried in Magnolia Cemetery;[189] married Ruby Lee McCauley.

   Norman Cloud McDill, born 23 March 1913;[190] died 3 October 1967 in Beaumont, Jefferson County, Texas, of coronary heart disease;[191] married Dorothy Broussard.

   Ray Nathaniel McDill, born 27 July 1917;[192] died 12 October 1974 in Orange County, Texas, due to a fall from ladder;[193] married Jean Delores Gordon.

High Steet, Belfast, 1786.

The port of Belfast as it must've looked to Nathaniel and his young family. Notice the ships in the harbor at the end of High Street, waiting to take passengers to America.

be discovered, by a number of enthusiasts, that old

Two views of Ballymena, the closest large town to Broughshane. Top: As it looked in the early 1800s, showing the old parish church (left) and the market house (right). Bottom: 1842, from the "fut o' th' town" viewing Bridge Street. The photos and descriptions were printed in the *Ulster Genealogical & Historical Guide*, Belfast, # 9, 1986.

Broughshane Village, Ballymena, Co. Antrim.

The village of Broughshane. The date of this picture is not known and there are no sure indicators of the time except for the horse and cart. My guess is about 1900. Some old sources say Nathaniel was born in Broughnow, a hamlet near Broughshane.

Slemish Mountain which may have been a familiar landmark to the McDill's in County Antrim.

Charleston Harbor as it appeared to Nathaniel McDill's family and to the other
McDills and Pedans in Reverend Martin's flotilla. This was their first
view of the New World.

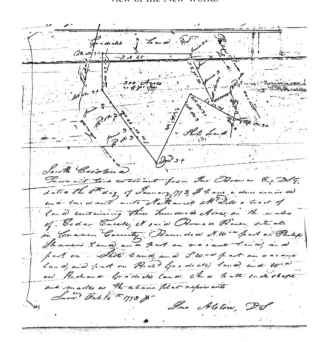

Plat of Nathaniel's original land grant, "waters of Cedar Creek,
north of Broad River." The double line at the top separates
Nathaniel's grant from the one preceding it.

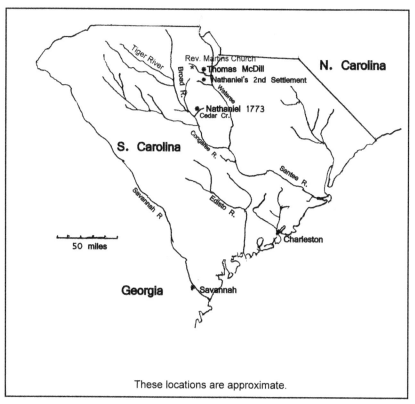

Tiger River

Rev. Martins Church

Thomas McDill

Nathaniel's 2nd Settlement

N. Carolina

Broad R.

Wateree

Nathaniel 1773

Cedar Cr.

Congaree R.

S. Carolina

Santee R.

Savannah R

Edisto R.

50 miles

Charleston

Georgia

Savannah

These locations are approximate.

This map shows the approximate location of Nathaniel's first land grant and the site of his second lands on Wateree Creek. The second site was much nearer his brother Thomas who had settled "on a branch of Rocky Creek."

An artist's rendering of a typical log schoolhouse on the Southern frontier.

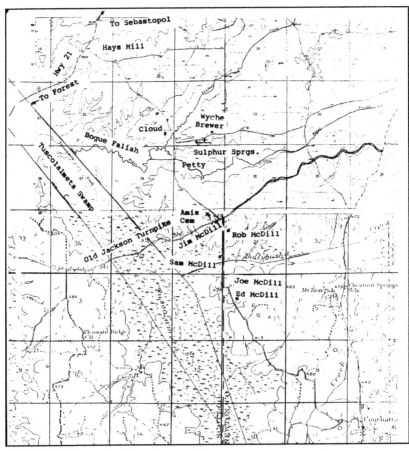

The locations of the McDill farms in Scott County, Mississippi, as well as the farms of several relatives. The map was made by Raymond Cloud Hunt, deceased.

The Ancestors and Descendants of Robert Nathaniel McDill

This is believed to be a picture of Ann McDill, wife
of Nathaniel McDill Jr., taken in the mid 1800s. Her
maiden name may have been Leslie or Logan.

Isabella McDill, wife of David Sargent. This is an
image on glass, probably taken in the early 1850s.

Thomas Alexander and Sarah Callahan (or Callaham) McDill, probably about 1892.

Thomas and Sarah McDill with their children at a family reunion in 1909. The children are placed according to age. The eldest son (back row, extreme right) is John William, nicknamed "Bud." Next is Thomas James who was called Jim. Moving left, Robert Nathaniel is next. Then comes Joseph Alexander who was called Joe, and Samuel Morris or Sam. The youngest, on the far left end, is Edward Wilder who was called Ed. The eldest daughter, Margaret Nazarene is seated on the far right in the front row. She was called "Sis." Next are Thomas and Sarah. Next to Sarah is Mary Jane who was called "Jenny." According to family lore, the empty chair was for Sarah Elizabeth who died in infancy in 1859. The youngest daughter, Ada Eugenia, is seated last in the row, on the far left end. Those in the picture were identified by Oneida McDill Herrington before her death, as told to Wayne V. McDill. She told the author on another occasion that "Poppa," (Robert Nathaniel) was recovering from pneumonia at the time. This picture has been repaired and "fussed over" through the years. In the original Robert Nathaniel was not wearing a tie.

Many thanks to my brother, Wayne, for interviewing Oneida McDill Herrington before her death in 1999 and having her identify the people in this photo. I assume this is the entire group in attendance at the 1909 family reunion. In a privately printed family photo album Wayne McDill stated:

> "On the top row, beginning at the right, is Jim McDill with his son Preston in his arms. Then comes Joe McDill holding Owen, who was crying and moved, blurring the long exposure shot. The third adult is Joe's wife, Allie. Next to Allie is the eldest of the McDill sons, John (Bud). The young man with the bowtie is Herbert Bishop, son of Josh and Margaret (Sis) Bishop. [Next] Eula Bea, at the center top, is John McDill's daughter. Sam McDill is the tallest one on the top row. Next to Sam is Victor McDill, eldest son of Jim and Annie. With his hair parted in the middle is Tom McDill, eldest son of John (Bud). The [next] young lady second from top is a daughter [not named] of John (Bud). The young man at top left is Rube, Rueben McDill, son of Jim and Annie. The man standing at the far left is Josh Bishop who married the eldest McDill daughter, Sis. Next to Josh Bishop is a boy about eight, his son Herman and a baby, probably Vernon, in his mother's arms, and his daughter Myrtle (in front of the baby). The girl in front of Josh Bishop with the large white ribbon in her hair is Gladys Burns, daughter of Bill and Jenny (the second McDill daughter).
>
> [In] The second row from the top, at the far right, is Annie McDill holding Kyle, the infant facing away from the camera. Others from right to left on the second row are: one of John's sons [not named], Maggie (Jim's daughter), Cleo (John's daughter), Veda (Jim's oldest daughter), Carrie Bishop, Mary McDill

The Ancestors and Descendants of Robert Nathaniel McDill

(John's eldest daughter) and her sister Eula Bea, Elvie Bishop, Ed McDill and his wife Brucie, who was expecting at the time.

The third row from the top seated, begins at the far right with Robert McDill with Oneida May on his lap with her hand over her mouth. She was three at the time... Next to Robert is his wife Dell with Marcus Alfred on her lap. He was one at the time. The third adult from the left seated is Mollie, wife of John McDill (Bud). Then comes grandpa McDill, Thomas Alexander and grandma, Sarah... Next to grandma was Ada Anderson, the youngest McDill daughter, holding James Morris McDill who was a few weeks old at the time. Three of the children at her feet are her boys Eugene, (plaid tie), Clyde, (leaning forward), and Mayo, (directly below the infant). The little dark-haired boy in their midst is Murphy McDill, a son of John. Alfred McDill, his brother, is the one in the sailor suit. The next woman on the third row is Mary Jane McDill Burns, with Norma, her youngest daughter, on her lap. To her right, holding up the baby, as already noted, is Mrs. Josh Bishop, the eldest McDill daughter.

On the second row from the front are the larger children. Beginning at the far right is Robert Clinton (called Clinton), the eldest son of Robert Nathaniel and Dell Cloud McDill, [who is] pictured just behind him. Second from the right is Sam McDill, son of John (Bud). Third is Edgar McDill, third son of Jim and Annie. Fourth, with his hair parted in the middle, is Malcolm McDill, son of John (Bud) and Mollie. The three girls in the center of this row are: Vera Burns, with the white ribbon in her hair, Bernice McDill, Bud's youngest daughter and Elsie Bishop.

The front row of children [all seated] are, beginning at the far right,... Herbert and Herman Bishop, Lindsay McDill, son of Jim and Annie [and] Audrey and Earnest McDill who were the children of Joe and Allie.

As already noted, the child in front dressed in what looks like a sailor suit is Alfred McDill, son of John (Bud). The other children near him have already been identified. At the far left front, [with her eyes] looking away to her right, is Elizabeth McDill (often called Lizzie), daughter of Jim and Annie. Next to her, the larger child with her hair pinned up, is Ozella Burns."

Samuel Morris McDill in about 1900.
That's quite a festive tie for such a serious
looking young man.

Joseph Alexander McDill in
about 1897, also sporting an
unusual neck tie.

Allie Hunt McDill, wife of Joseph McDill, in about 1905.

The Ancestors and Descendants of Robert Nathaniel McDill

Ada Eugenia McDill Anderson in about 1910.
Quite a perky young lady.

Dr. William Anderson, Ada Eugenia's husband,
taken at about the same time.

The Anderson children in about 1910. On the right is Eugene, the oldest. Mayo,
the second oldest is on the left and Clyde, the youngest is in the center.
They were identified for the author by Oneida McDill Herrington before her death.
She also stated that all three became medical doctors.

Another McDill family reunion held at the Ed McDill farm. After the death of Thomas (Grandpa McDill) these reunions were held on July 14, Sarah's birthday. That's Sarah on the right wearing a bonnet.

Thomas McDill's gravestone in the Methodist Churchyard Cemetery at Conehatta, Mississippi.

Sarah Callahan McDill's gravestone in the Methodist Churchyard

A rare photo of a middle aged Rob McDill. This and the picture of "Dell" demonstrate the early use of the "Kodak" or personal camera. Rob does not appear to be pleased.

Robert Clinton McDill in 1906 at the age of six, a classic portrait of the times.

The Ancestors and Descendants of Robert Nathaniel McDill

Guy Vernon McDill in 1910 or 1911.

Marcus Alfred McDill born 26 April
1909, died 17 may, 1911.

Norman Cloud McDill standing
behind the old Cloud house.

Oneida May McDill in 1909 at age
three. Notice the trick the photographer
used to make her appear
to be floating in air like an angel.

From left to right, Guy McDill, Oneida McDill Herrington and Norman McDill.

Walter Herrington, Oneida McDill Herrington and daughters.
Nancy Dell is on the left and Walterine is on the right.

The Ancestors and Descendants of Robert Nathaniel McDill

Family photo taken on the lawn of my childhood home in about 1947. Back row from left: Joyce McDill Ward, Phillip Ward, Guy McDill, Ray McDill, Dorothy Broussard McDill, Norman McDill, Oneida McDill Herrington and Walter Herrington. Front row from left: Walterine Herrington, Bob McDill, Wayne McDill, Thomas McDill and Nancy Dell Herrington.

Granddaddy Rob McDill with my brother Wayne, "Sissy" and "Nanny" Herrington in Mississippi. I was quite in love with my pretty Herrington cousins as a little boy.

"Miss Hattie" with the author in Texas in
about 1950. My mother claimed that Hattie
asked to be photographed standing behind a
bush because she was ashamed of her ankles.

"Miss Hattie and Mr. Rob" at the author's
childhood home in Texas. His legs
and eyesight were beginning to fail.

Norman McDill and Guy McDill with "Mr. Rob"
in Mississippi. Mr. Rob looks like a face on
Mount Rushmore.

Rob and Hattie at the "old home place" in Mississippi.

Robert Clinton McDill, the oldest of Rob and
Dell's children.

Guy Vernon McDill, my father.

Norman Cloud McDill

Staff Sergeant Ray McDill,
at the close of WW II.

My aunt, Oneida McDill, an
excellent school teacher.

Walter Herrington and Oneida McDill Herrington. Walt was my favorite uncle.

From left: Dorothy Broussard McDill, wife of Norman, Jean Gordon McDill, wife of Ray, Walter Herrington, Oneida McDill's husband, my mother, Ruby McCauley McDill, wife of Guy, and Phillip Ward, Joyce McDill Ward's husband. Joyce was of my generation, the daughter of Robert Clinton McDill.

Phillip Ward and Joyce McDill Ward.

Part Three:
Callaham aka
Callahan Genealogy

The Callaham Name

Early records of our line are consistent in using the spelling Callaham. It is an English name meaning one who came from Kellam (at the ridges) in Nottinghamshire.[1] Apparently, Sarah Callahan was the first to spell the name, or allow it to be spelled, Callahan. That name is, of course, Irish. In 1900, Sarah's mother Caroline was listed in the census as Caroline Callaham.[2]

Another possibility for the origin of the name exists in the records of the Daughters of the American Revolution. These indicate that David Calliham Sr. was born in 1726 in Scotland, married Elizabeth, and died 20 November 1789, in Georgia.[3] The record also states that he provided patriotic service to the Revolutionary cause in South Carolina. If he was indeed born in Scotland, then it is unlikely that he was the son of Nicholas and Joyce (Weaver) Callaham who are considered the progenitors of this line. They were residents of Surry County, Virginia, in 1723, three years before David's birth. However, the fact that he was born in Scotland suggests that there were Callahams in Scotland at an early date.

Morris Callaham
(~1693 – ~1721)

Morris Callaham may or may not have been the father of Nicholas Callaham who is generally recognized as the progenitor of this line. Morris must have been born no later than 1693 and probably earlier. In the fall of 1713, both Morris and (possible son) Nicholas Callaham registered their respective "crop marks" in Surry County, Virginia, at the same time. The record reads:

> *Upon the petition of Nicholas Callaham it is ordered that his mark being a crop and a nick under in the right ear and a flowerdeluce [sic] in the left be admitted to record. Under the petition of Morriss Callaham it is ordered that his mark being a crop and a slit and nick under in the right ear and a flowerdeluce in the left be admitted to record.*[4]

Farmers used ear cropping and branding to identify their hogs and cattle, as many of them roamed free and could mix with animals belonging to others.

Morris wrote his will on 19 December 1720 and it was probated in Surry County on 18 October 1721.[5] Witnesses were William Jones, William Malone, and Nicholas Callaham. He named a daughter Frances and a wife Frances, whom he also named as executrix. On 20 June 1722, Nicholas Callaham was named as the executor of his will.[6]

Possible children of Morris and Frances Callaham:
- Frances Callaham, born by December 1720, more likely about 1700.[7]
- **Nicholas Callaham,** born before 1693.

Nicholas Callaham
(~1693 – ~1752)

ℓ

Nicholas **Callaham** is considered the progenitor of the Callahams of America and specifically of Edgefield District, South Carolina. He was born in Virginia before 1693 and was married before 1719 to **Joyce Weaver**.[8] He died after 1752.[9] His wife Joyce was almost surely the daughter of John Weaver and his wife Elizabeth. John Weaver wrote his will in Surry County in 1719.[10]

In 1718, Nicholas bought a tract of land in Surry County, Virginia, from Robert Reeves.[11] On 5 September 1723, he patented (laid claim to) 350 acres in Surry County, on the south side of the Nottoway River and on "both sides of the Hunting Quarter at the swamp corner of John Anderson."[12] On 24 March 1725, he was listed as Nicholas "Callyham" when he patented another 270 acres in Surry County.[13] This tract was on the south side of the Nottoway River on Swing Swamp adjoining Hubbard Farrell's property by Rainey's Branch. He patented a third tract of 250 acres in Surry County on 22 September 1739.[14] This parcel was also located on the south side of the Nottoway River. It is described as "on the northwest side of the Hunting Quarter Swamp down the Cross Branch and adjoining Callyham's old line."[15] Hunting Quarter Swamp is located in the southern part of Sussex County, which was formed from Surry County, just south of the city of Sussex. Anderson Branch flows southerly to the west of Sussex and eventually into Hunting Quarter Swamp. This is probably the area where the Callahams lived.

On 15 March 1741/42, Nicholas Callaham's land was listed as adjoining that of John King and John Stephens. On that date, Stephens patented 450 acres in Surry County on the south side of Nottoway River and the south side of Hunting Quarter Swamp.[16]

On the same day, 15 March 1741/42, Nicholas patented 250 acres in Brunswick County on the North side of Kettle Stick Branch.[17] Brunswick

County was to the west of Surry County, but the Kettle Stick Branch location was a new one and it may have represented a move.

In December of 1741, Nicholas sold land in Surry County to John Stevens.[18] In January of 1747, "Nicholas Callaham of Surry County" sold a tract to John Shands.[19] Joyce, Nicholas's wife, was examined "privily" [privately] and relinquished her "dower right" or right as spouse to the land.[20] In March of 1750, Nicholas was living in Lunenburg County when he sold property to William Stuart of Surry County.[21]

On 15 December 1749, Nicholas patented another 400 acres, this time in Lunenburg County on the lower side of Flatt Rock Creek adjoining Freeman and Beal.[22] On the same day, 15 December 1749, he patented 190 acres in Surry County on the side of Nottoway River.[23] The tract began on the north side of the Hunting Quarter Swamp in a fork of the Wolf Pitt Branch "adjoining Callaham's other land."

On 21 August 1752, Nicholas was living in Cumberland Parish, Lunenburg County, when he deeded 250 acres to his son, John, of the same parish and county.[24] The deed stipulated that the land was to go to John after the death of Nicholas and his wife.

It isn't known exactly when Nicholas Callaham and his wife Joyce died. Over the years, Nicholas acquired over 1,700 acres in land patents alone. Since he married Joyce Weaver by 1719, and their known children, who are listed below, have birth dates between 1732 and 1740, it may be that these are only the youngest of the children.

Children of Nicholas and Joyce (Weaver) Callaham:

- David Callaham, born in Virginia; died 1784 South Carolina.

- **John Callaham**, born about 1732 in Surry County, Virginia; died 1804 in Lunenburg County, Virginia.

- Nicholas Callaham, born about 1736 Virginia; died about June 1797 in Lunenburg County, Virginia.

- Henry Weaver Callaham, born 21 April 1740 in Surry County, Virginia.

John Callaham
(~1732 – ~1804)
☙

John Callaham was born about 1732 in Surry County, Virginia, the son of Nicholas and Joyce (Weaver) Callaham.[25] His wife's name is unknown and since she is not named or mentioned in his will, she probably predeceased him.

On 1 August 1752, John Callaham received a gift from his father Nicholas of 250 acres on Kettlestick Branch in Lunenburg County.[26] This Lunenburg County deed proves that John was the son of Nicholas.

John wrote his will in Cumberland Parish, Lunenburg County, on 18 August 1803, and it was proved in court on 10 May 1804, in that County.[27] Witnesses to the will were William Garrett, Richard Garrett, and John Wyatt. Executors were Sterling Neblett, Morris Callaham, and Overstreet Wyatt.

The children listed below were named as heirs, except for David and Lightfoot who were already deceased. No widow was named in the will.

- Lightfoot Callaham; died 1777 (killed in service).[28]

- David Callaham, died before 13 September 1798, in Lunenburg County, Virginia.

- Frances "Fanny" Callaham; married Mr. Garrett.

- Joyce Callaham; married Sterling Mallett.

- Sarah "Sally" Callaham; married Mr. Scarborough, and had a daughter Jane Scarborough.

- Elizabeth Callaham; married Thomas Morgan.

- **Morris Callaham**; born about 1755 in Virginia; died in 1823 in Edgefield District, South Carolina.

The Ancestors and Descendants of Robert Nathaniel McDill

Morris Callaham
(~1755 – ~1823)
℃

Morris Callaham was born about 1755 in Virginia.[29] He married his first wife **Mary** by 1777.[30] His second wife **Jane** was born sometime after 1775, also in Virginia.[31]

Morris wrote his will on 19 January 1823, in Edgefield District, South Carolina.[34] This date is consistent with census records. He is buried at Calliham Mill Baptist Church in McCormick County, South Carolina. McCormick County wasn't formed until 1916 (from Greenwood and Abbeville counties). However, Greenwood County was formed in 1897 from Abbeville and Edgefield counties. Today, McCormick County forms the western boundary of Edgefield County, South Carolina. In his will, he named his widow Jane and nine children.

In 1830, the widow Jane Callaham was the head of the household in Edgefield District.[35] Three sons lived with her, two daughters aged fifteen to twenty, twenty-seven slaves, and an unnamed woman aged seventy to eighty.

Children of Morris and Mary Callaham:
- John Callaham, born 1794.

- Edmond W. Callaham, born 1794 to 1802; present in 1820.

Children of Morris and Jane Callaham:
- Elizabeth Callaham

- William Callaham, born 1802 to 1804; present in 1820.

- **Samuel W. Callaham**, born 1804–1811 in South Carolina present in 1820 and 1830.

- Sarah Callaham, born 1796–1800.

- Henry Callaham, born 1810–1815.

- James Callaham, born 1815–1820; with Jane in 1830.

- Mary Callaham, born 1810–1815.

- Jane Callaham, born 1810–1815.

Samuel W. Callaham
(~1811 – ~1900)

Samuel W. Callaham was born about 1811 in Edgefield District, South Carolina, the son of Morris and Jane Callaham.[36] He married **Caroline** who was born in 1822 in South Carolina, of parents born in South Carolina.[37]

In 1840, they were listed in the census of Edgefield District, South Carolina, with two girls under the age of five and three slaves in their household.[38] Samuel and Caroline appeared in the 1850 census of Edgefield County, South Carolina, with six children of their own and two children with the surname Cartlidge.[39] The census indicates that Samuel was thirty-nine, born in South Carolina, and was a farmer. He owned real estate valued at $1,200 plus 13 slaves.[40] Caroline was twenty-eight and also born in South Carolina, as were all their children.

By 1860, Samuel and Caroline were living in Newton County, Mississippi, but they had lingered in Alabama long enough to have two more children.[41] Samuel was listed in the census as blind. He owned no real estate but had personal property valued at $10,400, about $275,000 in 2010 dollars. The property may have been slaves.

Following the Civil War, the family is found living in Jasper County, Mississippi, with five children.[42] The financial loss caused by emancipation can be seen in their economic position. The slaves were gone, leaving them with real estate valued at $100.

In 1880, they were back in Newton County, living in Beat 3.[43] Samuel was about 69 years old and again listed as blind. Caroline was about 58. By 1900, Samuel had died and Caroline was living with her daughter, Clara Viola, who had married Enoch B. Edwards.[44]

Children of Samuel Callaham. Caroline may not have been the mother of the oldest children:

- **Sarah Elizabeth Callahan**, born 14 July 1837,[45] Edgefield District, South Carolina,[46] married on 15 December 1857 in Chambers County, Alabama, to **Thomas Alexander McDill.**[47] For more information, refer to the McDill section.

- Jane Callaham, born about 1838 in Edgefield District, South Carolina

- Morris Callaham, born about 1840, in Edgefield District, South Carolina.

- Irvin Callaham, born about 1847, in Edgefield District, South Carolina.

- Permelia "Mealy" Callaham, born in 1848, in Edgefield District, South Carolina.

- Olive Callaham, born in 1850, in Edgefield District, South Carolina; died by 1860.

- Frances Callaham, born about 1851, in Edgefield District, South Carolina.

- David Callaham, born about 1852, in Edgefield District, South Carolina.

- Patience E. Callaham, born about 1855 in Alabama.

- Millard F. Callaham, born about 1856 in Alabama.

- Clara Viola Callaham, born about 1863 in Mississippi.

- John Walter Callaham, born about 1863 in Mississippi.

- Charles P. Callaham, born about 1869 in Mississippi.

Part Four
Cloud Genealogy

The Cloud Name

The surname Cloud is believed to be either English or French.[1] It is an English topographic name given someone who lived near an outcrop or hill. In France, it was composed from a name borne by a saint and bishop in the sixth century. Despite the given name of descendant Marquis Lafayette Cloud, the Clouds are probably of English descent, since they are linked to others of English ancestry. Researcher Raymond Cloud Hunt speculated:

> William Cloud of Calne, Wiltshire, England came to America with the William Penn pilgrimage. He arrived in 1682 and with him were his sons Joseph, John, William Junior, Jeremiah and Robert. They settled in Chester County Pennsylvania. Descendents of William Cloud migrated down the eastern tear of states and the Cloud family in this book is probably descended from them.[2]

The Ancestors and Descendants of Robert Nathaniel McDill

Joseph Cloud Sr.
(~1725 – ?)

Ⓒ

Joseph Cloud Sr. was probably the progenitor of this line and father of Isaac Cloud senior. He settled in the southern part of Henry County, Virginia, and later purchased land in Rowan County, North Carolina (later Surry County), in 1755. It appears that he died in Stokes or Surry County.[3]

Isaac Cloud Sr.
(~1730 – ~1820)

ẽ

Isaac Cloud Sr. was born between 1730 and 1755.[4] He died after 1820, probably in Rutherford County, North Carolina.[5] His wife's name was Usley.[6]

He was listed as a taxpayer in Surry County, North Carolina, in 1782, along with Joseph Cloud and William Cloud.[7] On 4 May 1784, Isaac Cloud bought 200 acres on Elk Creek, "waters of Dan River" from William Woode and his wife Sarah for 100 pounds.[8] Witnesses were James Gaines, Daniel Ship, and Joseph Gaines.

On 3 November 1784, Isaac received a North Carolina land grant for 200 acres on Turkey Cock Creek.[9] On 11 August 1785, Isaac Cloud and his wife Usley sold the grant on Turkey Cock Creek to Thomas Smith of Henry County, Virginia, for forty pounds. Thomas Hickman, Phil Deatherage, and Joshua Hill were witnesses.[10]

Turkey Cock Creek is probably long since renamed. Turkey Cock Mountain, which is now known as Hen Mountain, is located in central Caldwell County, North Carolina.[11] This probably places the land in the northwestern portion of North Carolina.

In the North Carolina state census taken between 1784 and 1787, Isaac Cloud was listed in Surry County and was between the ages of twenty-one and sixty.[12] In his household were three males under twenty-one or above sixty and two females. Joseph Cloud also appears on the same census page.

In 1790, Isaac appeared in the census of Spartanburg County, South Carolina.[13] In his household were two males over sixteen, three under sixteen, and four females including his wife. This represents a move for Isaac and his family since as early as 1775, Surry County was on the northern boundary of North Carolina. Spartanburg is on the northern boundary of South Carolina adjoining Rutherford County, North Carolina, where Isaac eventually settled.

Isaac was quite a land speculator. On 5 May 1793, he received a 640-acre land grant in what would become Hawkins County, Tennessee.[14] Tennessee did not become a state until 1796. It seems unlikely Isaac ever lived on any of his land there. He was always listed as "of Rutherford County, North Carolina," when he sold his lands in Tennessee. However, many of his sons settled in Tennessee, some on the lands that he owned there.

On 13 May 1793, Isaac Cloud was in Rutherford County, North Carolina, when he sold the 200 acres on "Elk Creek waters" in Stokes County that he had purchased in 1784. The property was sold to Benjamin Cloud of Stokes County.[15] The land was identified as "where William Cloud now lives."

Between 1793 and 1795, Isaac Cloud sold slightly more than 587 acres in Hawkins County to various people, including his relatives.[16] Most tracts were identified as being on the north side of the Holston River. Poor Valley Creek was mentioned in some of them, a creek that is today located in Hawkins County.

When the 1800 census was taken, Isaac was living in Rutherford County, North Carolina.[17] He was over forty-five years of age. In his household were six apparent sons and at least four apparent daughters. The oldest female in his household was twenty-six to forty-five and could have been a younger wife or an older daughter.

On 16 December 1802, Isaac received grant #870 from North Carolina for 600 acres in Hawkins County,[18] which was located near the mouth of Fire Valley Creek.[19] On 3 December 1803, he sold 160 acres in Hawkins County near the mouth of Poor Valley Creek to Benjamin Cloud of Hawkins County.[20] In 1805, Isaac was again in Rutherford County, North Carolina, when he sold 120 acres in Hawkins County beginning at the "foot of the Knobbs," a local geographical landmark, to James Smith of Hawkins County.[21] The land adjoined that of John Henderson and Benjamin Cloud. A third grant, #2111, was issued by North Carolina to Isaac on 19 December 1811 for 50 acres.[22]

The last Hawkins County land transaction for Isaac was on 19 March 1808, when he sold 100 acres in Hawkins County to Mark Mitchell for $1,000.[23] The land was described as lying on the Holston River and known as Cobb's Island. Witnesses were Arthur Cobb, John W. Flowers Jr., and Isaac Cloud Jr. The deed was proven in court in Hawkins County in May 1810 by the oaths of the witnesses.

In 1810, Isaac Cloud again appeared in the census of Rutherford County.[24] He was over forty-five years old. Living with him were four sons under the age of sixteen and two women, one over forty-five and the other twenty-six to forty-five. Jesse Cloud, with a young wife and two sons under the age of ten, lived nearby.[25]

In 1820, Isaac Cloud Sr., Joel Cloud Esquire, and Jesse Cloud lived side by side in Rutherford County.[26] Isaac was the oldest of the three at forty-five plus years. Joel was probably more affluent as he was given the designation "Esquire." Isaac Cloud Jr. lived nearby.[27] Precisely when and where Isaac Cloud Sr. died remains a mystery.

Among the children of Isaac and Usley Cloud were:

❧ Joel Cloud, born 1775–1794.

❧ Jesse Cloud, born 1775–1794.

❧ **Isaac Cloud Jr.**, born about 1787 in South Carolina.[28]

Isaac Cloud Jr.
(~1787 – ~1855)

Isaac Cloud Jr. was born about 1787 in South Carolina,[29] the son of Isaac and Usley Cloud.[30] Isaac reportedly died on 17 August 1855 in Polk County, Tennessee.[31] His first wife's name is unknown, but his second was **Joanna** who was born in North Carolina in 1802.[32]

Isaac Jr. probably moved with his father to North Carolina. It was Isaac Jr., not his father, who first went to what is now Tennessee, although some of his brothers or relatives may have been there sooner.

Isaac Jr. must have married for the first time about 1808. He was not living with his father in 1810. It is now clear that he was living in Hawkins County, Tennessee, where he paid a "poll" or head tax.[34] The tax roll indicated that he owned no land. It could not have been referring to his father who would have been too old and exempted from the poll tax. The tax was usually levied on those 18 to 55 years old. In May of 1810, Isaac Jr. was in court in Hawkins County, Tennessee.[36] He gave his oath as a witness for the sale of land his father had owned.

In 1812, Isaac was taxed in Sullivan County.[37] By 1820, Isaac had returned to North Carolina where he was listed in the census of Rutherford County, living not far from his father.[38] He was twenty-six to forty-five years old with a wife in that same age bracket. There were five children in the household plus a woman over forty-five years of age.

Isaac married a second time in about 1830 to Joanna who was born in North Carolina in 1802.[39] It is assumed his first wife died. In 1840, he was living in Polk County, Tennessee, with a wife slightly younger than his first. This was surely Joanna. There was also a son aged ten to fifteen in the household and several apparent daughters.[40] Isaac was fifty to sixty years of age. On 3 February 1844, he was appointed to serve as an election judge in Civil District 5 of Polk County.[41]

In 1850, he lived in Murray County, Georgia, with his wife, Joanna, who was forty-eight years old.[42] Isaac's first-born son by his first wife, George, lived with them, as did Benjamin, a child by Joanna. In addition, there were four Carter children living in the household aged seven to ten years. John Carter was nine and Elizabeth was seven.

Isaac reportedly died on 17 August 1855 in Polk County, Tennessee, although no records survived in Polk County to prove this, and no source for the information has been located.[43] He was surely deceased by 1860 when Joanna was the head of the household in Catoosa County, Georgia.[44] She was fifty-one years old. Two Carter children were with her, a male J. aged nineteen and a female E. aged seventeen, presumably named John and Elizabeth.

Among the children of Isaac Cloud Jr. and his first wife whose name is unknown:

    ❧ George Washington Cloud, born about 1810 in Tennessee;[45] died 30 January 1861 in Polk County, Tennessee, and is buried in Rock Creek Cemetery, also known as Cloud Cemetery.[46] He married Dorinda A. Archer, born 13 January 1831, and died 28 February 1886.[47] An 1861 Polk County, Tennessee tax list referred to him as G.W. Cloud.[48]

    ❧ **James Madison Cloud**, born about 1817 in Tennessee.[49]

    ❧ Usley Cloud, born about 1820 in Tennessee; married on 2 March 1840 in McMinn County, Tennessee, to Elisha White.[50]

Among the possible children of Isaac Cloud Jr. and his second wife, Joanna:

    ❧ Benjamin Franklin Cloud, born in 1832 in Tennessee.[51] In Polk County, Tennessee, in 1861, listed as B. F. Cloud.[52]

The Ancestors and Descendants of Robert Nathaniel McDill

James Madison Cloud
(~1817 – ~1868)

James **Madison Cloud** was born about 1817 in Tennessee, the son of Isaac Cloud Jr.[53] He died in 1868 in Rapides Parish, Louisiana.[54] He married **Margaret "Peggy" King** in Murray County, Georgia, on 20 March 1838.[55]

James Cloud's name appeared on a delinquent tax list in Civil District 5 in Polk County, Tennessee, under the heading of 1844 to 1875. It indicated he had left the county.[56] His father, Isaac, still lived in the county at that time. In 1850, James resided in Murray County, Georgia, with his wife Margaret and five children.[57] His occupation was farmer and Warren Moss, age twenty-three, lived with him. In 1860, James and Peggy were back in Polk County, Tennessee, with all of their children.[58] In 1861, J. M. Cloud, B. F. Cloud, and George W. Cloud were on the tax list in Polk County, Tennessee.[59]

James Madison Cloud died in 1868 in Rapides Parish, Louisiana, and Margaret died in 1882 in Madison County, Mississippi.[60]

Children of James Madison and Margaret "Peggy" (King) Cloud:
- George Washington Cloud, born about 1839 in Murray County, Georgia; died 30 June 1861, and buried in Rock Creek Cemetery, Polk County, Tennessee.[61]

- **Marquis Lafayette Cloud**, born 22 December 1842 in Murray County, Georgia.

- Mary Jane Cloud, born about 1845, no issue.

- Seaborn Jefferson "Silas" Cloud, born 10 April 1847 in Polk County, Tennessee.

- Susan Margaret Cloud, born about 1849.

- Elizabeth Ellen Cloud, born about 1855, no issue.

- Benjamin Franklin Cloud, born about 1856.

- Sarah Jane Cloud, born about 1859, no issue.

- William Buchanan Cloud, born about 1860.

Marquis Lafayette Cloud
(~1842 – ~1902)

℃

Marquis Lafayette Cloud was born 22 December 1842,[62] in Murray County, Georgia, the son of James Madison and Margaret King Cloud.[63] He died 14 August 1902[64] in Scott County, Mississippi.[65] He married **Henrietta Virginia (Petty) Andrews** on 30 April 1874 in Scott County, Mississippi.[66]

In 1850, Marquis was listed in the census in his parent's household, and six years old.[67] This was probably the year the family moved to Polk County, Tennessee.[68]

The Civil War would be a principal event in Marquis' life. In March of 1861, Texas seceded from the Union, the last state to secede and join the Confederacy. A few days later, President Lincoln stated in his inaugural address that he would use the nation's full power to hold federal positions in the South. On April 12, the South fired on federally held Fort Sumter and forced its surrender. Lincoln called on Union troops to retake the Fort. The South considered this a declaration of war.

On 29 November 1861, Marquis, who was not quite nineteen years old, was mustered into the Confederate Army at Firestones, McMinn County, Tennessee. He served in Company A of the 59th Tennessee Infantry, known as Cooke's Regiment or Eakin's Regiment. They would later become mounted infantry or cavalry.[69] In October 1862, the 59th was reported in Brigadier General Henry Heath's Division, Colonel A. W. Reynolds's Brigade, which included the 3rd Confederate, 39th, 43rd, and 59th infantry regiments. These four Tennessee regiments remained together for the balance of the war.[70]

By 1862, the Union began to make plans to control the Mississippi River. Controlling the river would allow them to move arms and supplies into the heart of the Confederacy. The key to the Mississippi was Vicksburg. That city's guns guarded the river between Memphis and New Orleans. It was also heavily fortified. Grant tried several tactics, even attempting to dig a canal around the city so union troops and supplies could bypass Confederate cannon.

In December 1862, Marquis Cloud's brigade was moved to Vicksburg and put to use defending the city. Private Cloud was assigned to the crew of the famous Confederate rifled cannon, "Whistling Dick," in some accounts as a sharp shooter.[71] In his memoir, the chaplain at Vicksburg, William Lovelace Foster, stated: "Whistling Dick was a rifled, 18-pounder on the ramparts ... It became famous among Union and Confederate soldiers and sailors alike because of the distinctive whistling sound made by the projectiles fired."[72] It was also very effective.

Finally, in April 1863, Grant laid siege to the city. Several attempts were made to take the walls. A Confederate officer described one attack this way: "From that time our entire line became subjected to a murderous fire, and nearly every cannon on my line was in time either dismounted or otherwise injured. Assault with scaling ladders was made on the 22nd [May] and repulsed with heavy loss to Grant's troops."[73]

The city held out for six more weeks. Soldiers and citizens were near starvation. Civilians hid in caves to protect themselves from the shelling. Still casualties were high. Mules and horses were slaughtered for meat and some people were reduced to eating rats. Vicksburg surrendered on 4 July, the day after the Southern defeat at Gettysburg. Rev. Foster described his feelings in a letter after the city fell. Lamenting the closeness of Yankee gunboats, he said, "Poor whistling Dick will never have the pleasure again of sinking any of these monsters."[74]

Marquis was captured at the surrender of 4 July 1863. He was paroled on 9 July 1863 and gave his oath that he would not take up arms again until exchanged for a Union prisoner.[75] He was exchanged at Haines, Tennessee, on September 12, 1863.[76] In December, the 59th was mounted and served as cavalry for the balance of the war. On 31 January 1864, they were reported in Major General William T. Martin's Cavalry and on 31 March, in Major General Robert Ransom's Cavalry Corps. On 1 August 1864, they were part of General John Hunt Morgan's Cavalry or "Morgan's Raiders."[77] With Morgan, they engaged in several battles in Tennessee and Virginia.[78] In the last year of the war, Marquis was a brigade courier. He was captured by Michigan cavalry in the last days and was discharged in Virginia at the close of the war.[79]

According to family lore, young Marquis had suffered greatly during the siege of Vicksburg. Oneida McDill Herrington once stated: "Grandpa Cloud was so weak after the surrender that he had to be helped to his feet by his friends. All his life, he never really regained his health."[80]

In 1868, he moved to Mississippi, where in August 1877, he was baptized into the fellowship of Sulphur Springs Baptist Church by Brother Hudson.[81]

He married 30 April 1874, in Scott County, Mississippi, to Henrietta Virginia (Petty) Andrews,[82] a divorcee of whom his family disapproved.[83] Henrietta was born 28 June 1848, the daughter of John Wright and Christiana (Brewer) Petty.[84] For additional information, refer to the Petty section. Concerning the marriage, researcher Raymond Cloud Hunt wrote:

> She [Henrietta Virginia] first married (first name unknown) Andrews. They had one child, a female who did not survive infancy. Andrews left the country and deserted Virginia. After he was gone several years she got a divorce. When Dick and Virginia were married in 1874 both families were very upset because they felt a divorced woman was unfit. For a few years the couple lived away from the rest of the family in Newton County just to the east of Scott County. After some of the children were born they settled their differences and moved back near Virginia's family where Dick (Marquis Lafayette) patented a tract of land.[85]

In 1880, they lived in Scott County, Mississippi, with three young daughters.[86] Twenty years later, in 1900, they still lived in Scott County, but with seven children.[87] They lived two households from Henrietta's widowed mother Christiana Petty, three households from that of Robert Nathaniel McDill, whom their daughter "Dell" had married, and four households from Henrietta's brother, John W. Petty.[88] Also living with them was George Cloud, M. L. Cloud's sixty-year-old brother.

Marquis died 14 August 1902[89] in Scott County, Mississippi.[90] He is buried in Sulphur Springs Baptist Church Cemetery. In 1921, his wife received a pension based on his Confederate military service.[91]

In 1924, Henrietta moved with her "spinster" daughters May, Margaret D., and Leona, as well as her bachelor son William W. and her son James L. and his family to LaFeria, Cameron County, Texas.[92] She died there on 13 December 1925, and is buried in LaFeria Cemetery along with several of her children.[93]

Children of Marquis Lafayette and Henrietta Virginia (Petty) Cloud, probably all born in Scott County, Mississippi:

- Ada May Cloud, born 8 March 1875; died 6 January 1955 in La Feria, Cameron County, Texas, no issue.

- **Lida Adella "Dell" Cloud**,[94] born 24 June 1877; died 19 June 1928; married Robert Nathaniel McDill. For additional information, see the McDill family section.

- Margaret Drummond "Maggie" Cloud, born 11 November, 1879; died 19 December 1964 in La Feria, Texas, no issue.

- James Lafayette Cloud, born 13 January 1881; died 27 April 1947 in La Feria, Texas; married Emma Anderson.

- Leona Belle Cloud, born 14 May 1883, no issue.

- Ethel Cloud, born 9 November 1886; died 12 November 1886.

- Johnnye Blanche Cloud, born 14 December 1887; died 15 May 1973 in McAllen, Texas; married James Singleton Hunt.

- William Wright Cloud, born 12 October 1891; died 11 October 1980 in La Feria, Texas, no issue.

- Flora Virginia Cloud, born 13 March 1895; died 27 March 1913, no issue.

Part Five
Petty aka
Pettit/Pettus Genealogy

The Petty/Pettus Name

Information about early generations of the Pettus family is taken from several sources.[1] However these sources offer little proof. Reportedly, Thomas Pettus, the English progenitor of the family, was born about 1519 and died 7 January 1597. He was sheriff and mayor of Norwich, England, and is buried at St. Simon and Jude Church where a monument is erected in his memory on the South side of the chancel arch. In 1591, he purchased the manor of Rackneath from William Holmes.[2]

His eldest son, Sir John Pettus of Norwich, inherited the manor and the title Baronet. His successors lived there until the male line became extinct in England in 1772. For another five generations of this family see *Extinct and Dormant Baronetcies of England* by John Burke, London, 1838.

John's younger brother was Thomas or Thomas of Norwich who was baptized on 17 September 1552, and married Cecily King. Among their children was William Pettus who was baptized on 12 August 1583 and died 19 December 1648. He reportedly married Mary Gleane and among their children was Thomas Pettus who was born about 1609.

It is interesting to note that Henry Pettus, author of one of the sources on the family, comments in his 1966 genealogy that he found no further record of the family after he traced them to Essex County, Virginia, where Thomas's son Thomas died about 1665.[3] He wonders what became of them. This is easy to explain. The surname changed from Pettus to Pettit, which the author noted, but he lost track of the family when the surname changed again, to Petty.

The Ancestors and Descendants of Robert Nathaniel McDill

Thomas Pettus aka Pettit
(~1609 – ~1665)

Thomas Pettus aka Pettit was born about 1609, the son of William and Mary (Gleane) Pettus. He was known to be a large landowner and "an outstanding man." Thomas owned land on Hoskins Creek in Rappahannock County, Virginia.[4] He married **Katherine Morris**, the daughter of Major George and Eleanor Morris.[5]

Apparently Thomas had an uncle of the same name who was only ten years his senior. Reportedly one of the two was indicted for manslaughter in 1629 in England and was later released due to efforts by his family. The same man was again indicted for a felony in 1631. At that time, his family had him sent to a "distant place." Which Thomas Pettus this was is unclear. But according to one source, the uncle was on the Continent serving the Crown in the Thirty Years War at the time.[6] The Thomas Pettus who, a few years later, was sent to Virginia to oversee a land grant owned by Sir John Pettus is also believed to be the uncle. Where the "distant place" was is anyone's guess. But the whereabouts of our Thomas, the nephew, between 1631 and his arrival in Virginia in 1643 are unknown. This leads us to assume he was the man earlier indicted. In any event, in that year, he obtained lands in Rappahannock County.[7]

Apparently he repaired his reputation by the time of his death, and was considered "an outstanding man." He wrote his will in the name of Thomas Pettit in Rappahannock County, Virginia, on 23 September 1663, and it was probated in June 1665.[8] His wife Katherine is named in his will, although his daughter Dorothy was his sole heir. He left her "the land I now live on" which consisted of 280 acres by conveyance, plus a 100-acre patent. According to his will, Thomas's wife was to live on the land as long as she remained single. Nicholas White and Thomas Cooper were named as friends and executors. Witnesses were Richard Glover and Richard Martingale.

Thomas and Katherine had one additional child who was not named in his will, a son, Thomas, born in the spring after the death of his father.[9] Katherine apparently did not remain single. She married a second time to John Long and a third to Thomas Gaines.[10]

Children of Thomas and Katherine (Morris) Pettit:
- Dorothy Pettit, born about 1655 married first, after 1675, to James Fugett and second to Godfrey Stanton.[11] Dorothy was still single in 1675 when her father's friend, Thomas Cooper, named her in his will as Dorothy Pettit.[12] He left her a cow.

- **Thomas Pettit**, born about May or June 1665.

Thomas Pettit aka Petty
(~1665 – ~1720)

Thomas Pettit aka Petty was born about 1665 in Rappahannock County, Virginia, the son of Thomas and Katherine (Morris) Petty. He married **Rachel Wilson**.[13]

When he wrote his will on 18 November 1719, he stated that he was of Southfarnham Parish in Essex County.[14] It was probated 17 May 1720 under the name of Thomas Pettit. In it he named his wife Rachel and six children. In the will, he mentioned land in King and Queen Counties. The inventory of his estate amounted to over 230 pounds and included ten slaves valued at 172 pounds.

Children of Thomas and Rachel (Wilson) Pettit aka Petty:

- George Petty

- **Thomas Petty**, born about 1680 in Essex County, Virginia.

- Benjamin Petty

- Rachel Petty

- Elizabeth Petty

- Mary Petty

- Rebecca Petty; married by 1748/1749 to Thomas Simms.

- Mary Petty; married by 1748/1749 to Knight.

- George Petty, born about 1716, married a Simms.

- Martha Petty; unmarried at the writing of his will.

Thomas Petty
(~1680 – ~1750)

℃

Thomas Petty was born about 1680 in Essex County, Virginia, reportedly the son of Thomas and Rachel (Wilson) Petty.[15] He married **Catherine Garton**, daughter of John and Martha Garton.[16] In 1737, in Orange County, Virginia, where Thomas had relocated, he was excused from work on the road due to his advanced age, which would have been about fifty-seven.[17] Able-bodied young men were obligated to work on the roads or send some one in their stead. Thomas Petty was now excused.

Thomas wrote his will on 31 January 1748/1749 and it was probated in April 1750 in Orange County, Virginia.[18] He made no provision for his wife, so she is presumed to have predeceased him. While he apparently named all of his children in his will, he left only a shilling to most of them and divided his estate between his son George and his daughter Martha, making them executor and executrix. Thomas Petty was now excused.

Children of Thomas and Catherine (Garton) Petty:

- John Petty, born about 1702, married Rebecca Simms.

- **Thomas Petty Jr.**, born in 1704 in Orange County, Virginia.

- Christopher Petty, born about 1708.

- William Petty, born about 1709; son Theophilus Petty, born by June 1735[19] and son William, born by August 1741.[20]

- James Petty, born about 1715.

Thomas Petty Jr.
(~1704 – ?)

℮

Thomas Petty Jr. was born in 1704 in Orange County, Virginia, the son of Thomas and Catherine (Garton) Petty.[21] On 24 August 1727, he married **Elizabeth Moore**, daughter of Francis and Ann (Harbin) Moore.[22]

On 2 June 1735, he was listed as Thomas Petty Jr. when he received a lease for life for 150 acres in Orange County from Alexander Spotswood, Esquire. The lease was for the lives of William Petty, identified as Thomas Jr.'s son, and Theophilus Petty, identified as his brother William's son.[23] This was probably done to lengthen the lease. The land was described as being on the south side of the Rapidanne, part of 40,000 acres granted Alexander Spotswood called the Spotsylvania Tract.

On 25 August 1741, the executors of Alexander Spotswood executed another lease of 150 acres in St. Mark's Parish, Orange County, this time to William Petty, Thomas Jr.'s brother, for the lives of William's sons, William and Theophilus Petty.[24] This land was located north of the Rapidanne, part of the same 40,000-acre tract.

On 26 March 1739, Alexander Spotswood leased 100 acres in St. Marks's Parish to Harbin Moore for the lives of Harbin Moore and Francis Petty, son of Thomas Petty Jr.[25] There is a logical explanation for this lease. Thomas Jr.'s wife Elizabeth was nee Moore and her mother was nee Harbin, so Harbin Moore was surely Elizabeth's brother. Harbin probably selected his young nephew, Francis Petty, to be on the lease to extend its length. When and where Thomas Jr. died is unknown.

Children of Thomas Jr. and Elizabeth (Moore) Petty:
- ❧ Francis Moore Petty, born 27 June 1728; died 1816, served in the American Revolution; married Mary. Will recorded 26 February 1816.

The Ancestors and Descendants of Robert Nathaniel McDill

ᴥ **William Petty**, born about 1730; married Elizabeth.

ᴥ Ann Petty, born 1732.

ᴥ Lovey Petty, born 1734.

ᴥ Elizabeth Petty.

William Petty
(~1730 – ~1805)

W illiam Petty was born about 1730, perhaps in Lunenburg County, Virginia, the son of Thomas Jr. and Elizabeth (Moore) Petty.[26] He married **Elizabeth,** whose maiden name is unknown, in about 1754.[27] William provided patriotic service in the state of Virginia during the American Revolution.[28] He was a surveyor and was licensed to own a tavern.

William wrote his will on 27 September 1804.[29] He died in Clark County, Kentucky, by 27 May 1805 when it was probated. In it, he named his wife **"Lettis"** and, presumably, all of his sons and daughters. Lettis may have been what he called Elizabeth. But some have speculated that Lettis was a second wife.[30] Elias Petty, who reportedly married Elizabeth Martin, is listed in the *Cloud Family of Scott County, Mississippi,* but not named in his will.

Children of William and Elizabeth Petty:

- Elizabeth Petty, married Dodson.

- Rachel Petty, married Russell.

- Hannah Petty, married Ward.

- Zachariah Petty

- **William Eli Petty,** born 13 March 1764,[31] probably in Fauquier County, Virginia.[32]

- Randell Petty

- John Petty

- James Petty

- Sarah Petty, married Stevens.

- Rhoda Petty, married first to Elisha Cast and second to Thomas Taylor.

- Francis Petty

- Thomas Petty

William Eli Petty
(~1764 – ~1834)

𝒞

William Eli Petty was born 13 March 1764,[33] probably in Fauquier County, Virginia, the son of William and Elizabeth Petty.[34] He married **Lucretia "Lucy" Wright** about 1783.[35] She was the daughter of John and Ann (Williams) Wright.[36] Lucy was born 7 July 1765,[37] in Fauquier County.[38]

They moved to Surry County, North Carolina, by 1790. At sixteen, William enlisted in the Continental Army.[39] He served as a private in Captain Boswick's company under the command of Colonel Armstrong.[40] After the war, he moved to Wilkes County, North Carolina, and in 1815, to Madison County, Alabama, where he patented land in 1815.[41] On 29 October 1832, in Madison County, he applied for and received a pension based on his service in the Revolution.[42]

William died on 26 September 1834 in Madison Co. and is buried there.[43] Lucy died 16 August 1842 and is buried next to her husband.[44] He was a farmer.

Children of William Eli and Lucretia "Lucy" (Wright) Petty:

ᨀ Nancy Petty, born 28 February 1785, died 26 December 1846, in Coffee County, Tennessee; married John Dickerson.

ᨀ Eli Williams Petty, born 26 December 1786, died 1 July 1854; married Diane Martin Harrison.

ᨀ Lazarus Petty, born 7 July 1779, died 1 July 1844; married Sarah.

ᨀ **John Wright Petty**, born 28 February 1791; married Ann Harris.

ᨀ Zachariah Petty, born 23 May 1792, died 8 July 1854; married Rebecca Shackleford.

- Amelia Petty, born 20 July 1795, died 1869; married David Carlton

- William Thornton Petty, born 29 September 1797; married Abigail Bayless.

- Sally Petty, born 11 August 1799.

- James William Petty, born 12 October 1801; married Elizabeth Morgan.

- Thomas Merce Petty, born 5 October 1803.

- Benjamin Franklin Petty, born 4 November 1805; married Cynthia Bryan and Jane Nesbit.

- Daniel Harrison Petty, born 28 February 1812.

John Wright Petty
(~1791 – ~1876)

ℰ

John Wright Petty was born 28 February 1791 in Wilkes County, North Carolina, the son of William Eli and Lucretia "Lucy" (Wright) Petty. He was a physician. In about 1815, he married **Anna Harris**, the daughter of Sarah Harris of Montgomery County, North Carolina. Anna was born 18 January 1798 and died 13 June 1869. She is buried in Foster Cemetery in Madison County, Alabama.[45]

In her history of Dr. John Wright Petty Jr.'s ancestry, Genealogist Alice Hodges wrote:

> *There is on record in Madison County Alabama, a deed of gift from Sarah Harris of Montgomery County, North Carolina to "beloved daughter" Ann Harris and John Wright Petty, her husband, of two slaves. This deed was filed 17 February 1823.*[46]

In 1850, John and Anna lived in Madison County, Alabama, with five of their children and a granddaughter, Ann Mitchell, who was eight years old.[47] He was listed as a doctor, aged fifty-nine, and Ann was fifty-two.

John Wright Petty Jr. died 23 September 1876 and is buried in Madison County, Alabama.

Children of John Wright Petty and Anna (Harris) Petty:

- Dewitt Cinton Petty, born 1817 in Lincoln County, Alabama.

- William W. Petty, born 1819.

- Albert Gallatin Petty, born 29 May 1820; died 2 June 1879; married Luvenia Brewer, born 11 February 1825.

- Sarah A. Petty; married Eli Mitchell; probably died by 1850, leaving daughter Ann Mitchell born 1842.

- **John Wright Petty Jr.**, born 12 November 1824 in Madison County, Alabama; married Christiana Brewer.

- William Howard Petty, born 1825; married Margaret Norris.

- Nancy Petty, born 26 January 1826; died 26 December 1846, never married.[48]

- Ann Eliza Petty, born 1828.

- Richard P. Petty, born 8 January 1829; married Margaret Norris?

- Daniel Boone Petty, born about 1830, never married.

- Cornelia Petty, born about 1833, never married.

- Lucretia "Lucy" Petty, born about 1835.

- Newton Eli Petty, born about 1838, never married.

John Wright Petty Jr.
(~1824 – ~1858)

℃

John **Wright Petty Jr.** was born 12 November 1824 in Madison County, Alabama, the son of John Wright and Anna (Harris) Petty. In about 1848, he married **Christiana Brewer,** daughter of Wyche and Flora (McPherson) Brewer.[49] Christiana was born about 1827 in Alabama.[50]

Raymond Cloud Hunt related that, "About 1845 he [John Wright Petty Jr.] moved to Sumter County, Alabama with his brother Albert Gallatin Petty. There, they met their wives, the daughters of Wyche Brewer. A few months after the Brewer family moved to Scott County, Mississippi the brothers followed them and got married."[51]

In 1850, the young couple lived in Scott County, Mississippi, with their daughter Henrietta, who was two years old at the time. They were two households from Christiana's parents.[52]

John Wright Petty Jr. died 27 March 1858 in Scott County, Mississippi, and is buried in the Amis Cemetery. In 1860, his widow Christiana, age thirty-three, lived with her four children next door (according to the census taker) to her parents in Scott County.[53] She owned real estate valued at $1,500 and personal property worth $500.

In 1880, Christiana, aged fifty-three, was the head of the household in Beat 5, Scott County.[54] She lived next door to her daughter, Henrietta (Petty) Cloud. In 1900, Christiana was seventy-three and still head of a household in Scott County with her daughter Flora, who was forty-seven.[55] Christiana probably died in Scott County after 1900.

Children of John Wright and Christiana (Brewer) Petty, all named in the 1860 census:

    ❧ **Henrietta Virginia Petty**; married Marquis Lafayette Cloud. See the Cloud section for further information.

- William Wright "Albert" Petty, born 1851; died at Harpersville, Mississippi; married Mary Millsap, no issue.

- Flora Ann Petty, born 30 September 1852; died 26 September 1935, never married.

- John William Petty, born 26 November 1854; died 22 December 1936; married Emma Wall.

Sarah Callahan (or Callaham) McDill. This old photo had serious water damage. I did the best I could with it.

The Ancestors and Descendants of Robert Nathaniel McDill

Christiana Brewer Petty in about 1867. She was "Dell" Cloud's grandmother and my great, great grandmother.

A later picture of Virginia Petty Cloud. This was probably an early "Kodak" since it was taken outdoors and the quality in not particularly good.

Marquis Lafayette "Dick" Cloud in about 1890.
This portrait was made from a tintype in the
possession of Oneida McDill Herrington.
It appeared to have been carried in a wallet or
purse for many years.

Virginia Petty Cloud in about 1890. She was
"Dell" Cloud's mother and my great grandmother.

The only recognizable adult photo of "Dell" Cloud McDill known to exist. This is a "Kodak" taken behind the old Cloud house around 1920.

A studio portrait of Jane Cloud, younger sister of "Dick" Cloud, taken in about 1880. This may be either Sarah Jane or Mary Jane.

James Lafayette Cloud, younger brother of Dell in about 1905. He headed up the Cloud family party that moved from Mississippi to take up new lands in south Texas in the 1920s.

The pretty little Cloud sisters in about 1882. On the left is Margaret Dee, in the center, Ada May and on the right, Lida Adella or "Dell."

Ada May Cloud in about 1900. She was one of eight
children of Marquis Lafayette and Virginia Petty Cloud.
Five of the eight siblings never married, including Ada.

John William "Will" Petty and his daughters in
about 1895. William was Henrietta Virginia Petty
Cloud's brother and the husband of Hattie Wall's sister,
Emma. On the far left is Nina, on the right is Lila,
and in the foreground, Fanny.

Notes

Part 1

1. George F. Black, *The Surnames of Scotland: Their Origin, Meaning and History* (New York: New York Public Library, 1946), 486.
2. Ibid.
3. Letter dated 22 February 1983 from the Scottish Tartans Society to Bob McDill (Nashville, Tennessee), copy held in 2010 by McDill.
4. Ibid.
5. Clan MacDowall, electricscotland.com/webclans/m/2.html (8/6/2012)
6. Ian Moncreiffe and Don Pottinger, *Clan Map: Scotland of Old* (Edinburgh: John Bartholomew & Son, Ltd.), Approved by the Standing Council of Scottish Chiefs and by the Lord Lyon King of Arms.
7. *Burke's General Armory* (London: 1884), 639.
8. Ibid.
9. Fergus Macdowall & William MacDougall, *The MacDowalls* (Canada: Clan Macdougall Society of North America, 2009), xi. The authors list the Lyon Court, Edinburgh as source.
10. George Way of Plean and Romilly Squire, *Scottish Clan and Family Encyclopedia* (New York: HarperCollins Publishers, 1994), 219.
11. Ibid.
12. Ibid.
13. Histories-MacDowall of Galloway, rampantscotland.com/clans/blclanmacdowall.htm (8/6/2012)
14. Fergus D. H. Macdowall and William L. MacDougall, *The MacDowalls* (Clan MacDougall Society of North America, 2009), 133.
15. Daphne Brooke, *Wild Men and Holy Places* (Edinburgh: Canongate Press, 1994), 2.
16. Lloyd Laing, *Celtic Britain* (London: Rutledge and Kegan Paul, 1979), 25.
17. Way and Squire, *Scottish Clan and Family Encyclopedia*, 218.
18. Peter and Fiona Fry, *The History of Scotland* (New York: Barnes & Noble, 1982), 25.
19. Fry, *The History of Scotland*, 28.
20. Brooke, *Wild Men and Holy Places*, 3.
21. Ibid., 5.
22. Leo McDowell, My McDowell Family, leomcdowall.tripod.com/id31.html (8/6/2012)
23. Charles MacKinnon, *Scottish Highlanders* (New York: 1992), 174–5.
24. David Ross, *Scotland History of a Nation* (New Lanark, Scotland: Geddes & Grosset) 50.
25. A. S. Mather, Scotland, *World Book Encyclopedia* (Chicago, Illinois, 2000).
26. Fry, *The History of Scotland*, 46.
27. Ibid., 49.
28. Brooke, *Wild Men and Holy Places*, 1.
29. Ibid.
30. Ibid., 82.
31. Fitzroy MacLean, *Scotland A Concise History* (London: Thomas & Hudson, 1970), Fry, The History of Scotland, 62.

32. G.W.S. Barrow, *Kinship and Unity, Scotland* c. 1000–1306 (London: University of Toronto Press, 1981), 11–12.
33. Fry, 78.
34. Way and Squire, *Scottish Clan and Family Encyclopedia*, 218.
35. Ross, 89.
36. John Prebble, *The Lion in the North: a Personal View of Scotland's History* (London: Taylor & Francis, 1971), 92.
37. Ronald McNair Scott, *Robert The Bruce* (New York: Random House, Inc., 1982), 212.
38. Ibid.
39. Web posting, *Electric Scotland*, Clan MacDowall.
40. David Ross, 125.
41. Macdowall & MacDougall, 13.
42. Ibid.
43. Black, *The Surnames of Scotland: Their Origin, Meaning and History*, 487.
44. In 1525, the Earl of Angus and members of the Douglas Clan kidnapped the then thirteen-year-old King James V of Scotland and seized power In 1526, Gilbert Kennedy, the Earl of Cassilis, joined the Earl of Arran in a failed attempt to rescue the King. This presumably involved an armed force and possibly there were casualties. In 1528, James managed to escape and regain power.

    There may be another explanation for the arrests. In 1526, the Earl of Cassilis, along with his son-in-law, Fergus M'Douall, and their retinue went to attend Parliament in Edinburgh. They met another party, possibly the Stewartry of Galloway, on the Royal Mile and an argument broke out about who would yield to the other. It turned into a melee resulting in several deaths. This theory about the reason for the arrests was proposed to me by Fergus Day Hort Macdowall, our Clan Chieftan.
45. Black, *The Surnames of Scotland: Their Origin, Meaning and History*, 486.
46. Ancestry.com, McDill surname, Distribution of McDill Families.
47. Leyburn, *The Scotch-Irish a Social History* (Chapel Hill, North Carolina: University of North Carolina, 1962), 3.
48. Ross, 176.
49. Leyburn, *The Scotch-Irish a Social History*, 33.
50. Ibid., 4.
51. Ibid., 7.
52. Thomas Hobbs, *Leviathan*, Part I, chapter 13.
53. Leyburn, *The Scotch-Irish a Social History*, 11.
54. Prebble, *The Lion in the North: a Personal View of Scotland's History*, 191.
55. Leyburn, *The Scotch-Irish a Social History*, 91.
56. Ibid.
57. Leyburn, *The Scotch-Irish a Social History*, 93.
58. Ibid.
59. Leyburn, *The Scotch-Irish a Social History*, 94.
60. Robert Bell, *The Book of Ulster Surnames* (Belfast: 1988), 155.
61. April 1984 letter from Ulster Historical Foundation, 66 Balmoral Avenue, North Ireland to Bob McDill (Nashville, Tennessee).
62. Leyburn, *The Scotch-Irish a Social History*, 105. James Webb, *Born Fighting, How the Scots-Irish Shaped America* (New York, 2004), 85–86.

63. Jonathon Bardom, *A History of Ulster* (Belfast: Blackstaff Press, 1992), 175–176.

64. Dickson, *Ulster Immigration to Colonial America 1718–1785* (London: 1966), 75.

65. Bardom, *A History of Ulster*, 207–208.

66. Johnson, *A Journey to the Western Islands of Scotland* (New York: 2002), 110.

67. Bardom, 209–210.

68. Leyburn, *The Scotch-Irish a Social History*, 173.

69. Ibid., 173.

70. Dickson, *Ulster Immigration to Colonial America 1718–1785*, 97.

71. David Hackett Fischer, *Albion's Seed* (Oxford, England: 1989), 614.

72. Leyburn, *The Scotch-Irish a Social History*, 175.

Part 2

1. This information is found in LDS [Mormon] undocumented records and also in *McDills* (see below). Both are questionable sources, but are included here since there are insufficient Irish records to prove or disprove the statements. This applies to all of the information on John, his wife, and his children except where otherwise footnoted.

2. Robert McDill Woods and Ivey Godfrey Woods, *McDills in America* (Ann Arbor, Michigan: Edward Brothers, Inc., 1940), 3. It is believed the Woods' source was a family Bible.

3. Jonathan Bardon, *A History of Ulster* (Belfast, Northern Ireland: Blackstaff Press Ltd., 1992), 158.

4. Ibid.

5. Woods, *McDills in America*, 3.

6. The Woods book stated that Thomas and Margaret were both born near Broughshane, Ballymena Parish. But Broughshane is in Racavan Parish. I simply deleted that detail from the entries for Thomas and Margaret. However the book did have the correct parish for its information on Nathaniel.

7. Ann Collins and Louise Knox, editors, *Heritage History of Chester County, South Carolina* (Chester, South Carolina: privately published, 1982), 353.

8. Woods, *McDills in America*.

9. Ibid.

10. Ibid., 3.

11. Ibid., 3.

12. *Kershaw County, South Carolina, Volume 1:67*, wills not recorded, will #778.

13. Nathaniel McDill will, *Kershaw County, South Carolina, Volume 1:67*, wills not recorded, will #778. His widow was Mary.

14. Widow McDill household, 1790 U.S. census, Camden District, Chester County, South Carolina, 186.

15. Woods, *McDills in America*, 3.

16. Ibid. Leyburn, *The Scotch-Irish a Social History*, 105. James Webb, *Born Fighting*,

17. Woods, *McDills in America*, 122.

18. C. Donnelly, 13 March 1985 letter, Ulster Historical Foundation, to B. McDill (Nashville, Tennessee), 1.

19. C. Donnelly, 13 March 1985 letter, 1.

20. Arthur Herman, *How the Scots Invented the Modern World* (New York: Three Rivers

Press, 2001), 120.

21. Dickson, *Ulster Emigration to Colonial America 1718–1785* (London: Routledge & Regan Paul Ltd., 1966), 74.

22. Jean Stephenson, *Scotch-Irish Migration to South Carolina, 1772* (Strasburg, Virginia: Shenandoah Publishing, 1971), 19.

23. Ibid.

24. Ancestry.com, Belfast newsletter, December 31, 1771, page 3 (11/19/13).

25. Myer, *Descendants of John McDill and Jane Bell, Belfast, Ireland*, microfilm 599201 Family History Library, Salt Lake City Utah.

26. Woods, *McDills in America,* 163.

27. Stephenson, *Scotch-Irish Migration to South Carolina, 1772*, 27–28.

28. Dickson, *Ulster Immigration to Colonial America 1718–1775*, 248.

29. Ibid.

30. Ancestry.com, 4 Apr. 2009. History, John Pedan.

31. Stephenson, *Scotch-Irish Migration to South Carolina, 1772*, 30–31.

32. Woods, *McDills in America,* 122.

33. Dickson, *Ulster Immigration to Colonial America 1718–1775*, 206.

34. Ibid., 207.

35. Stephenson, *Scotch-Irish Migration to South Carolina, 1772*, 33.

36. Ibid., 31.

37. Ibid., 30.

38. Ibid., 74.

39. South Carolina Council Journal, 6 January 1773, co/5/507, 13–14, South Carolina Department of Archives and History, Columbia, South Carolina.

40. Stephenson, *Scotch-Irish Migration to South Carolina, 1772*, 74.

41. Ibid.

42. *South Carolina Grant Book* 24:410, 10 May 1773.

43. Chester County, South Carolina, deeds, Plat Book 18–199, Grant Book 24–410.

44. David Hackett Fischer, *Albion's Seed, Four British Folkways in America* (Oxford University Press, New York, 1989), 729.

45. Grady McWhiney, *Cracker Culture* (Tuscaloosa, Alabama: University of Alabama Press, 1988), 56.

46. Robert Frost, "The Mending Wall," *North of Boston* (Henry Holt & Co., 1917).

47. Fischer, 728.

48. Fischer, 729.

49. *Memorials, Volume 12*, 146, South Carolina Department of Archives and History, Raleigh, South Carolina.

50. Brent Holcomb, *South Carolina Deed Abstracts 1783–1788* (Columbia, South Carolina: privately printed), 1996.

51. Gelee Corley Hendrix and Morn McKoy Lindsay, *The Jury Lists of South Carolina 1778–1779* (Greenville, South Carolina: privately printed, 1975), 51.

52. Brent Holcomb, *South Carolina's Royal Grants Volume Four: Grant Books 25 through 31 1772–1775* (Columbia, South Carolina: SCMAR, 2009), 264.

53. Ancestry.com posting, John Pedan, History: the first plat is described in Plat

Folder 1482, Pre-Revolutionary Plats.

54. Stephenson, *Scotch-Irish Migration to South Carolina, 1772*, 20.
55. Ibid.
56. *Kershaw County, South Carolina, Volume 1:67*, wills not recorded, will #778. His will indicated that his land was on Wateree Creek.
57. Moss, *Roster of South Carolina Patriots in the American Revolution*, 671.
58. Ibid., 614.
59. Southern Campaign Revolutionary War Pension Applications and Rosters, pension application of John McDill S21879.
60. *Kershaw County, South Carolina, Volume 1:67*, wills not recorded, will #778.
61. Widow McDill household, 1790 U.S. census, Chester County, South Carolina, Camden District, 186.
62. Nat Medill [sic] household, 1800 U.S. census, Fairfield County, South Carolina, 178.
63. Myer, *Descendants of John McDill and Jane Bell*, Belfast, Ireland, microfilm 599201 Family History Library, Salt Lake City Utah.
64. While no source was found for this date, it is probably close to correct since his wife was a widow in the 1860 census. He was known to die in Tallapoosa County as his estate papers were filed there in 1871.
65. There is no source for Ann's surname, but she was identified as Ann in Nathaniel's estate papers. No early marriage records were maintained in South Carolina and the marriage date is estimated from the births of their first children.
66. David Sargent household, 1860 U.S. census, Chambers County, Alabama, southern division, sheet 70, stamped p. 953B, dwelling and family 483. Ann lived with them in 1860, but this does not prove her surname was Leslie.
67. 1871 loose records estate of Nathaniel McDill filed under the name of James McDill, Tallapoosa County, Alabama, probate court, copy held in 2011 by compiler Shirley Wilson (106 Leeward Point, Hendersonville, TN 37075).
68. Widow McDill household, 1790 U.S. census, Chester County, South Carolina, Camden District, 186.
69. Ibid.
70. Nat Medill [sic] household, 1810 U.S. census, Fairfield County, South Carolina, 178.
71. Nathaniel McDill household, 1820 U.S. census, Abbeville County, South Carolina.
72. Coweta County, Georgia, *Deed Book F:35*, microfilm 473253, Family History Library, Salt Lake City, Utah.
73. Nathanial McDill household, 1840 U.S. census, Coweta County, Georgia, stamped p. 318, second family from top of page.
74. Nathaniel McDill household, 1850 U.S. census, Coweta County, Georgia, division 19, stamped p. 375B, dwelling and family 1318.
75. Myer, *Descendants of John McDill and Jane Bell, Belfast, Ireland*, microfilm 599201 Family History Library, Salt Lake City Utah.
76. *World Book Encyclopedia*, Volume A, 276.
77. Coweta County, Georgia, *Deed Book I-311*, microfilm 70–4, Georgia Archives, Atlanta, Georgia.
78. Tallapoosa County, Alabama, *Deed Book G:55–56*; microfilm 1304522, Family

History Library, Salt Lake City, Utah.

79. Half of a section is 320 acres.
80. Tallapoosa County, Alabama, *Deed Book G:46–57*; microfilm 1304522, Family History Library, Salt Lake City, Utah. History Library, Salt Lake City, Utah.
81. Estate of Nathaniel McDill filed under the name of James McDill, Tallapoosa County, Alabama, probate court, copy held in 2011 by compiler Shirley Wilson (106 Leeward Point, Hendersonville, TN 37075). 81
82. Nath. McDill household, 1855 Tallapoosa County, Alabama, state census, 26.
83. MariLee Beatty Hageness, Marriages 1835–1869, *Tallapoosa County, Alabama* (no place: privately published, 1994), 81.
84. While there is no known source for this date, it is probably close to correct since his wife was a widow in the 1860 census. He was known to die in Tallapoosa County as his estate papers were filed there in 1871.
85. David Sargent household, 1860 U.S. census, Chambers County, Alabama, southern division, sheet 70, stamped p. 953B, dwelling and family 483.
86. 1871 loose records estate of Nathaniel McDill filed under the name of James McDill, Tallapoosa County, Alabama, probate court, copy held in 2011 by compiler Shirley Wilson (106 Leeward Point, Hendersonville, TN 37075).
87. She was in named in estate papers as Georgia Ann but in the census as Georgiana.
88. N. L. McDill household, 1860 U.S. census, Coosa County, Alabama, 2nd Subdivision, stamped p. 347, dwelling and family 863.
89. 1871 loose records estate of Nathaniel McDill filed under the name of James McDill, Tallapoosa County, Alabama, probate court, copy held in 2011 by compiler Shirley Wilson (106 Leeward Point, Hendersonville, TN 37075).
90. Ibid.
91. Letter dated 11/02/13 from Louise McDill of Manchester Tennessee in the possession of Bob McDill.
92. 1820 census Abbeville South Carolina, ancestry.com (11/17/13).
93. *Coweta County, Georgia, Marriages 1827–1979*, 79.
94. 1871 loose records estate of Nathaniel McDill filed under the name of James McDill, Tallapoosa County, Alabama.
95. Ibid.
96. Ibid.
97. Lois Tessmer Strebeck, *Newton County, Mississippi, Cemeteries Volume 1* (Ozark, Missouri: Dogwood Printing, 1993), irregular pagination, p. 3 of section on Connehatta Methodist Church Cemetery.
98. 1871 loose records estate of Nathaniel McDill filed under the name of James McDill, Tallapoosa County, Alabama. Also Chambers County, Alabama, marriages, 435a.
99. Nathaniel McDill household, 1850 U.S. census, Coweta County, Georgia, division 19, stamped p. 375B, dwelling and family 1318.
100. N. L. McDill household, 1860 U.S. census, Coosa County, Alabama, 2nd Subdivision, stamped p. 347, dwelling and family 863.
101. 1871 loose records estate of Nathaniel McDill filed under the name of James McDill, Tallapoosa County, Alabama.
102. N. L. McDill household, 1860 U.S. census, Coosa County, Alabama, 2nd

Subdivision, stamped p. 347, dwelling and family 863.

103. Hageness, *Marriages* 1835–1869, Tallapoosa County, Alabama, 81.

104. 1871 loose records estate of Nathaniel McDill filed under the name of James McDill, Tallapoosa County, Alabama.

105. Nathaniel McDill household, 1850 U.S. census, Coweta County, Georgia, division 19, stamped p. 375B, dwelling and family 1318.

106. 1871 loose records estate of Nathaniel McDill filed under the name of James McDill, Tallapoosa County, Alabama.

107. Tombstone photograph, held in 2010 by Robert McDill (Nashville, Tennessee). Also Strebeck, Newton County, Mississippi, Cemeteries, Volume 1, p. 3 of section on Connehatta Methodist Church Cemetery.

108. 1871 loose records estate of Nathaniel McDill filed under the name of James McDill, Tallapoosa County, Alabama, probate court, copy held in 2011 by compiler Shirley Wilson (106 Leeward Point, Hendersonville, TN 37075).

109. Tombstone photograph, held in 2011 by Bob McDill, (Nashville, Tennessee). Also Strebeck, *Newton County, Mississippi, Cemeteries,* Volume 1, p. 3 of section on Connehatta Methodist Church Cemetery.

110. Sarah was the first to spell her name Callahan not Callaham. The reason is not known.

111. Chambers County, Alabama, marriages, 435a.

112. Strebeck, *Newton County, Mississippi, Cemeteries,* Volume 1, p. 3 of section on Connehatta Methodist Church Cemetery.

113. Mrs. Sarah McDill, death certificate #14249 (1933), Mississippi State Board of Health. This proved her date of birth and that her father was a Callahan, but it does not name her mother and her place of birth is listed as Alabama. S. W. Calliham 1850 U.S. census, Edgefield District, South Carolina, stamped p. 79, dwelling and family 1212. This lists a daughter Sarah age 11. In 1900, Newton County, Mississippi Beat 3, sheet 18, stamped p. 249B Caroline Callaham is listed as a widow living just a few doors from her married daughter, Sarah Elizabeth Callaham McDill.

114. Mrs. Sarah McDill, death certificate #14249 (1933), Mississippi State Board of Health.

115. Nathanial McDill household, 1840 U.S. census, Coweta County, Georgia, stamped p. 318, second family from top of page.

116. James McDill household, 1850 U.S. census, Abbeville District, South Carolina, Savannah River Reg., stamped p. 63, dwelling and family 980.

117. Tallapoosa County, Alabama, Deed Book G:r455–456, microfilm 1304522, Family History Library, Salt Lake City, Utah.

118. Ibid.

119. Thomas McDill household, 1855 Tallapoosa County, Alabama, state census, 23–24.

120. James McDill household, 1855 Tallapoosa County, Alabama, state census, 18.

121. Nath. McDill household, 1855 Tallapoosa County, Alabama, state census, 26.

122. Tallapoosa County, Alabama, Deed Book Z:334–335; microfilm 1769648, Family History Library, Salt Lake City, Utah.

123. U.S. grant #13260 issued 1 March 1858 to Thomas A. M. Dill, Bureau of Land Management on-line database.

124. Chambers County, Alabama, marriages, p. 435a. Also Mrs. Sarah McDill, application for pension (widows) filed 4 April 1930 from Mississippi. Copy held

in 2011 by Robert L. McDill (Nashville, Tennessee).

125. Ibid.

126. Mrs. Sarah McDill, death certificate #14249 (1933), Mississippi State Board of Health. This proved her date of birth and that her father was a Callahan, but it does not name her mother and her place of birth is listed as Alabama. S. W. Calliham 1850 U.S. census, Edgefield District, South Carolina, stamped p. 79, dwelling and family 1212. This lists a daughter Sarah age 11. In 1900, Newton County, Mississippi Beat 3, sheet 18, stamped p. 249B Caroline Callaham is listed as a widow living just a few doors from her married daughter, Sarah Elizabeth Callaham McDill.

127. Tallapoosa County, Alabama, *Deed Book M:233–234*; microfilm 1304525 Family History Library, Salt Lake City, Utah.

128. This was an error. It should read the southwest quarter of the southwest quarter.

129. Tallapoosa County, Alabama, *Deed Book M:285–286*; microfilm 1304525 Family History Library, Salt Lake City, Utah.

130. Samuel Calahan [sic] household, 1860 U.S. census, Newton County, Mississippi, Hickory P.O., stamped p. 727, dwelling 237, family 248.

131. Thomas McBell [sic] household, 1860 U.S. census, Newton County, Mississippi, Hickory post office, p. 727, dwelling 238, family 249, The Callahams lived at dwelling 237, family 248.

132. Thomas A. McDill Confederate Service Record, War Department Collection of Confederate Records, National Archives, Washington, DC.

133. Ibid.

134. Mrs. Sarah McDill, application for pension (widows) filed 4 April 1930. Copy held in 2010 by Bob McDill (Nashville, Tennessee).

135. Thos. A. McDill household, 1870 U. S. census, Newton County, Mississippi, Newton Township, p. 55, stamped p. 412B, dwelling and family 10.

136. Thomas A. McDill Confederate Service Record, War Department Collection of Confederate Records, National Archives, Washington, DC.

137. Ibid.

138. Ibid.

139. As told by Guy V. McDill to Bob McDill (Nashville, Tennessee).

140. Thomas L. Connelly, *Autumn of Glory, The Army of Tennessee, 1862–1865* (Baton Rouge: L.S.U. Press, 1971), 506.

141. Connelly, *Autumn of Glory, The Army of Tennessee, 1862–1865*, 511.

142. Laura Edwards, "The McDill Family of Coosa and Tallapoosa Counties, Alabama," *Tap Roots*, Volume 47, No. 4, April 2010.

143. Tallapoosa County, Alabama, Deed Book Z:334–335; microfilm 1769648 Family History Library, Salt Lake City, Utah.

144. Thos. A. McDill household, 1870 U. S. census, Newton County, Mississippi, Newton Township, p. 55, stamped p. 412B, dwelling and family 10.

145. Bess Hollingsworth, Land Records of Newton County, Mississippi, 1883, 13.

146. Thomas A. McDill household, 1900 U.S. census, Newton County, Mississippi, Beat 3, enumeration district 52, sheet 18, stamped p. 249B, dwelling 318, family 326.

147. Photograph of tombstone, Methodist Church Cemetery, Conehatta, Mississippi. Photo held in 2011 by Bob McDill (Nashville, Tennessee).

148. Sarah M. McDill household, 1910 U. S. census, Newton County, Mississippi,

Beat 3, sheet 7, stamped p. 99, dwelling and family 90.

149. Mrs. Sarah McDill, death certificate #14249 (1933), Mississippi State Board of Health.

150. Lindon E. Brown, *Bits and Pieces, From Conehatta to Heaven's Gate* (place not named: Nelson Printing, 2011).

151. Thos. A. McDill household, 1870 U. S. census, Newton County, Mississippi, Newton Township, p. 55, stamped p. 412B, dwelling and family 10. Also Strebeck, Newton County, Mississippi, Cemeteries Volume 1, p. 3 of section on Conehatta Methodist Church Cemetery.

152. Thos. A. McDill household, 1870 U. S. census, Newton County, Mississippi, Newton Township, p. 55, stamped p. 412B, dwelling and family 10.

153. Ibid.

154. William Harold Graham, Newton County, Mississippi, Marriage Records, 1872–1952, 235.

155. Ibid.

156. R. N. McDill marriage to Adella Cloud, Scott County, Mississippi, *Marriage Book 4:588*; microfilm 899206, Family History Library, Salt Lake City, Utah.

157. T. A. McDill household, 1880 U.S. census, Newton County, Mississippi, Beat 3, stamped p. 604.

158. Thomas A. McDill household, 1900 U.S. census, Newton County, Mississippi, Beat 3, enumeration district 5–2, sheet 18, dwelling 318, family 326.

159. Letter dated 11/02/13 from Louise McDill of Manchester Tennessee in the possession of Bob McDill.

160. Sarah M. McDill household, 1910 U. S. census, Newton County, Mississippi, Beat 3, sheet 7, stamped p. 99, dwelling and family 90.

161. Thomas A. McDill household, 1900 U.S. census, Newton County, Mississippi, Beat 3, enumeration district 5–2, sheet 18, dwelling 318, family 326.

162. Newton County, Mississippi, Marriage Records, 1872 1952, 235.

163. Thomas A. McDill household, 1900 U.S. census, Newton County, Mississippi, Beat 3, enumeration district 5–2, sheet 18, dwelling 318, family 326.

164. Thos. A. McDill household, 1870 U. S. census, Newton County, Mississippi, Newton Township, p. 55, stamped p. 412B, dwelling and family 10. Also information from grandson Bob McDill (Nashville, Tennessee).

165. Information supplied by grandson Bob McDill (Nashville, Tennessee) to compiler Shirley Wilson (106 Leeward Point, Hendersonville, Tennessee), February 2010.

166. R. N. McDill marriage to Adella Cloud, Scott County, Mississippi, Marriage Book 4:588; microfilm 899206, Family History Library, Salt Lake City, Utah.

167. Marcus Cloud household, 1880 U.S. census, Scott County, Mississippi, Beat 5, stamped p. 101, dwelling 70, family 75. Also Marquis Lafayette Cloud, Confederate military service record, Company A and C, 59th Tennessee Mounted Infantry, Tennessee State Library and Archives, Nashville, Tennessee. Mrs. M.L. Cloud (Virginia) application for widow's pension dated 27 June 1924 Scott County, Mississippi. Virginia identified her husband as Marquis Lafayette Cloud in this document.

168. *Cloud Family of Scott County, Mississippi*, probably by Raymond Cloud Hunt. (no place, privately printed, no date), 9.

169. Although the marriage and birth dates were found among the genealogy collection

The Ancestors and Descendants of Robert Nathaniel McDill

of Rob's grandson, Bob McDill (Nashville, Tennessee), the marriage record was not found in the Newton County courthouse.

170. Thos. A. McDill household, 1870 U. S. census, Newton County, Mississippi, Newton Township, p. 55, stamped p. 412B, dwelling and family 10.

171. Personal comments in this biographical sketch from Robert Nathaniel McDill's grandson Bob. McDill (Nashville, Tennessee).

172. R. N. McDill marriage to Adella Cloud, Scott County, Mississippi, Marriage Book 4:588; microfilm 899206, Family History Library, Salt Lake City, Utah. Also *Cloud Family of Scott County, Mississippi*, 9.

173. Robert N. McDill household, 1900 U.S. census, Scott County, Mississippi, Beat 5, tamped p. 145, dwelling 166, family 170.

174. Robert N. McDill household, 1910 U. S. census, Newton County, Mississippi, Beat 3, sheet 12, stamped p. 104, dwelling and family 176.

175. As related to Bob McDill by various family members, no death certificate could be found.

176. Robert N. McDill household, 1930 U.S. census, Newton County, Mississippi, Beat 3, District 12, stamped p. 111B, dwelling 117, family 119.

177. Bob McDill (Nashville, Tennessee) obtained this information from an unknown source, although the actual marriage record was not located in Newton County.

178. Zachariah Wall household, 1900 U.S. census, Newton County, Mississippi, Beat 3, stamped p. 250B, dwelling 322, family 330.

179. Information supplied by grandson (Bob McDill, Nashville, Tennessee) to compiler Shirley Wilson (106 Leeward Point, Hendersonville, Tennessee), February 2010.

180. Bob McDill (Nashville, Tennessee) obtained this information from Laura C. Edwards of Raleigh, North Carolina.

181. Robert N. McDill household, 1900 U.S. census, Scott County, Mississippi, Beat 5, stamped p. 145, dwelling 166, family 170.

182. Robert C. McDill death certificate #38535 (1959), Texas Bureau of Vital Statistics.

183. Robert N. McDill household, 1910 U. S. census, Newton County, Mississippi, Beat 3, sheet 12, stamped p. 104, dwelling and family 176.

184. Related to Bob McDill by Walterine Herrington Bell 18 Apr. 2012.

185. William Harold Graham, Newton County, Mississippi, Marriage Records, 1872–1952, 235.

186. Ibid.

187. Robert N. McDill household, 1930 U.S. census, Newton County, Mississippi, Beat 3, District 12, stamped p. 111B, dwelling 117, family 119.

188. Guy Vernon McDill death certificate #95771 (1973), Texas Bureau of Vital Statistics.

189. Ibid.

190. Norman Cloud McDill death certificate #66779 (1967), Texas Bureau of Vital Statistics.

191. Ibid.

192. Ray Nathaniel McDill death certificate #94204 (1974), Texas Bureau of Vital Statistics.

Part 3

1. Elsdon C. Smith, *New Dictionary of American Family Names* (New York: Gramercy Publishing Company, 1988), 71.
2. S. W. Calliham household, 1850 U.S. census, Edgefield County, South Carolina, stamped p. 79, dwelling and family 1212.
3. *DAR Patriot Index, Centennial Edition, Part 1* (Washington, DC: Daughters of the American Revolution, 1990), 473.
4. Weynette Parks Haun, *Surry County, Virginia, Court Records 1712–1718 Book VII* (Durham, North Carolina: privately printed, 1993), 44.
5. Davis, *Wills and Administrations of Surry County, Virginia, 1671–1750*, 26.
6. Ibid.
7. Ibid.
8. *Descendants of Nicholas Callaham*, no author, downloaded from Family Tree Maker's Genealogy Site <Genealogy Report: Descendants of Nicholas Callaham> 29 June 2010 by Shirley Wilson. Also Eliza Timberlake Davis, Wills and Administrations of Surry County, Virginia, 1671–1750 (Baltimore: Genealogical Publishing Company, 190), 139. There is no proof that he was born in Virginia or that he was NOT born in Virginia.
9. June Banks Evans, *Lunenburg County, Virginia, Deed Book 3 1752–1754* (New Orleans: Bryn Flyliaid Publications, 1990), 23.
10. Eliza Timberlake Davis, *Wills and Administrations of Surry County, Virginia, 1671–1750* (Baltimore: Genealogical Publishing Company, 190), 139. His will named a daughter Joyce Calliham.
11. Haun, *Surry County, Virginia, Court Records 1712–1718 Book VII*, 106.
12. Nell Marion Nugent, *Cavaliers and Pioneers, Abstracts of Virginia Land Patents and Grants, Volume III* (Richmond, Virginia: Virginia State Library, 1979), 254.
13. Ibid., 307.
14. Nugent, *Cavaliers and Pioneers, Volume IV*, 204.
15. Ibid.
16. Nugent, *Cavaliers and Pioneers, Volume V*, p. 12.
17. Nugent, *Cavaliers and Pioneers, Volume V*, p. 13.
18. Weynette Parks Haun, *Surry County, Virginia Court Records 1741–1745* (Durham, North Carolina: privately printed, 1995), 1.
19. Weynette Parks Haun, *Surry County, Virginia Court Records 1749–1751* (Durham, North Carolina: privately printed, 1997), 81.
20. In Virginia, the wife had a life or dower interest in any land her husband owned during their marriage. When the land was sold, she was examined apart from her husband to make certain that she freely relinquished her dower interest.
21. Haun, *Surry County, Virginia Court Records 1749–1751*, 97.
22. Nugent, *Cavaliers and Pioneers, Volume VI*, 2.
23. Nugent, *Cavaliers and Pioneers, Volume VI*, 3.
24. June Banks Evans, *Lunenburg County, Virginia, Deed Book 3 1752–1754* (New Orleans: Bryn Flyliaid Publications, 1990), 23.
25. Evans, *Lunenburg County, Virginia, Deed Book 3 1752–1754* (New Orleans: Bryn Flyliaid Publications, 1990), 23. The patent to Nicholas for this land identified it as in Brunswick County.
26. Evans, *Lunenburg County, Virginia, Deed Book 3 1752–1754* (New Orleans:

Bryn Flyliaid Publications, 1990), 23. The patent to Nicholas for this land identified it as in Brunswick County.

27. June Banks Evans, *Lunenburg County, Virginia, Will Book 6 1802–1809* (New Orleans: Bryn Flyliaid Publications, 1992), 29.

28. *Lunenburg County, Virginia, Will Book* 3:8.

29. Descendants of Nicholas Callaham.

30. Ibid.

31. Morris Calliham [sic] household, 1820 U.S. census, Edgefield District, South Carolina, p. 101A. S. W. Callihan [sic] household, 1880 U.S. census, Newton County, Mississippi, Beat 3, enumeration district 37, stamped p. 603B proves parents born in Virginia.

32. 1790 U.S. census, Edgefield District, South Carolina, 570.

33. 1800 U.S. census, Edgefield District, South Carolina, 167B.

34. Morris Calliham [sic] household, 1820 U.S. census, Edgefield District, South Carolina, p. 101A.

35. *Abstracts of Wills of Edgefield County, South Carolina* (Albany, Georgia: Delwyn Associates, 1973), 70.

36. Jane Callaham household, 1830 U.S. census, Edgefield District, South Carolina, 136.

37. While there is no one fact that proves this, Samuel is their son by process of elimination as there were no other Callaham families in Edgefield County from 1820 to 1850 except for Morris and Jane. Also Descendants of Nicholas Callaham names him as a son. Also he named his first daughter Jane and his first son Morris.

38. Marriage date based on the birth date of their first child in 1838, see 1850 census entry. S. W. Callihan [sic] household, 1880 U.S. census, Newton County, Mississippi, Beat 3, enumeration district 37, stamped p. 603B proves her parents' place of birth.

39. S. W. Callaham [indexed as S. W. Callikam], 1840 U.S. census, Edgefield County, South Carolina, stamped p. 90.

40. S. W. Calliham household, 1850 U.S. census, Edgefield County, South Carolina, stamped p. 79, dwelling and family 1212. Also: 1859 US Federal Census-Slave Schedules, SW Callaham, Ancestry.com (17/11/13).

41. Samuel Calahan [sic] household, 1860 U.S. census, Newton County, Mississippi, Hickory P.O., stamped p. 727, dwelling 237, family 248.

42. Samuel W. Calliham [sic] household, 1870 U.S. census, Jasper County, Mississippi, North Beat, stamped p. 551, family 535.

43. S. W. Callihan [sic] household, 1880 U.S. census, Newton County, Mississippi, Beat 3, enumeration district 37, stamped p. 603B.

44. Enoc [sic] B. Edwards household, 1900 U.S. census, Newton County, Mississippi, Beat 3, stamped p. 249B.

45. Strebeck, *Newton County, Mississippi, Cemeteries Volume 1*, p. 3 of section on Connehatta Methodist Church Cemetery. Also Mrs. Sarah McDill, death certificate #14249 (1933), Mississippi State Board of Health. This proves her date of birth. She stated that her father was a Callahan, but it does not name her mother.

46. S. W. Calliham [sic] 1850 U.S. census, Edgefield District, South Carolina, stamped p. 79, dwelling and family 1212. This lists a daughter Sarah age 11. In

1900, Newton County, Mississippi Beat 3, sheet 18, stamped p. 249B Caroline Callaham is listed as a widow living just a few doors from her married daughter, Sarah Elizabeth Callaham McDill.

47. Chambers County, Alabama, marriages, 435a.

Part 4

1. Patrick Hanks and Flavia Hodges, *Dictionary of Surnames* (Oxford: Oxford University Press, 1991), 113.
2. Raymond Cloud Hunt, *Ancestors and Descendents of Marquise Lafayette Cloud & Henrietta Virginia Petty* (McAllen, Texas: privately published, 1987) 1.
3. Hunt, 2F.
4. Isaac Cloud household, 1800 U.S. census, Rutherford County, North Carolina, 101.
5. Isaac Cloud household, 1820 U.S. census, Rutherford County, North Carolina, 382.
6. Ibid., 91.
7. Clarence Ratclifff, *North Carolina Tax Payers 1679–1790* (Baltimore: Genealogical Publishing Company, 1987), 40.
8. Mrs. W. O. Absher, *Surry County, North Carolina, Abstracts of Deed Books A, B. & C* (1770–1788) Easley, South Carolina: Southern Historical Press, 1981), 65.
9. Absher, *Surry County, North Carolina, Abstracts of Deed Books A, B. & C*, 81.
10. Ibid., 91.
11. William S. Powell, *The North Carolina Gazetteer* (Chapel Hill, North Carolina: University of North Carolina Press, 1968), 222.
12. Mrs. Alvaretta Kenan, *State Census of North Carolina 1784–1787* (Baltimore: Genealogical Publishing Company, 1987), 151.
13. Isaac Cloud household, 1790 U.S. census, Spartanburg County, South Carolina, 28.
14. Isaac Cloud grant #314 dated 5 May 1793, Hawkins County, Tennessee, North Carolina Book 3:191.
15. *Cloud Family of Scott County, Mississippi*, 18. Copy held in 2011 by Bob McDill (Nashville, Tennessee), citing DB 3:13 Stokes County, North Carolina.
16. Hawkins County, Tennessee, Deed Book 2:93, 136149, 257, 284; microfilm 33, Tennessee State Library and Archives, Nashville, Tennessee.
17. Isaac Cloud household, 1800 U.S. census, Rutherford County, North Carolina, 101.
18. Isaac Cloud grant #870 dated 16 December 1802, Hawkins County, Tennessee, North Carolina Book C:409.
19. Joyce Martin Murray, *Hawkins County, Tennessee, Deed Abstracts 1801–1819* (Dallas, TX: privately printed, 1998), 56.
20. Murray, *Hawkins County, Tennessee, Deed Abstracts 1801–1819*, 58.
21. Ibid., 70.
22. Isaac Cloud grant #2111 dated 19 December 1811, Eastern District Grant Book 3:300.
23. *Hawkins County, Tennessee, Deed Book* 6:351, microfilm 35, Tennessee State

Library and Archives, Nashville, Tennessee.

24. Isaac Cloud household, 1810 U.S. census, Rutherford County, North Carolina, 10.

25. Jesse Cloud household, 1810 U.S. census, Rutherford County, North Carolina, 93.

26. Isaac, Jesse, and Joel Cloud households, 1820 U.S. census, Rutherford County, North Carolina, 382.

27. Isaac Cloud Jr. household, 1820 U.S. census, Rutherford County, North Carolina, 380.

28. Isaac Cloud household, 1850 U.S. census, Murray County, Georgia, stamped p. 150B, dwelling 40.

29. Ibid.

30. Absher, *Surry County, North Carolina, Abstracts of Deed Books A, B. & C*, 91. This deed proves his mother's given name as Usley. He also names a daughter Usley.

31. Polk County, Tennessee, minutes 1840 to 1866, the only records that exist in that time period, were searched for the period of his stated death with negative results.

32. Isaac Cloud household, 1850 U.S. census, Murray County, Georgia, stamped p. 150B, dwelling 40.

33. Byron and Barbara Sistler, *Early Tennessee Tax Lists* (Evanston, Illinois: Byron Sistler and Associates, 1977), 38.

34. Pollyanna Creekmore, *Early East Tennessee Taxpayers* (Easley, South Carolina, Southern Historical Press, 1980), 72.

35. Ibid.

36. *Hawkins County, Tennessee, Deed Book* 6:351, microfilm 35, Tennessee State Library and Archives, Nashville, Tennessee.

37. Sistler, Early Tennessee Tax Lists, 38.

38. 38 Isaac Cloud Jr. household, 1820 U.S. census, Rutherford County, North Carolina, 380.

39. Isaac Cloud household, 1850 U.S. census, Murray County, Georgia, stamped p. 150B, dwelling 40.

40. Isaac Cloud household, 1840 U.S. census, Polk County, Tennessee, 14.

41. WPA Polk County, Tennessee, Court Minutes 1844–1847, p. 6, referencing original minutes, 137.

42. Isaac Cloud household, 1850 U.S. census, Murray County, Georgia, stamped p. 150B, dwelling 40.

43. Polk County, Tennessee, minutes 1840 to 1866, the only record that exists in that time period, were searched for the period of his stated death with negative results.

44. J. Cloud household, 1860 U.S. census, Catoosa County, Georgia, p. 17, stamped p. 1003, dwelling 557, family 539.

45. Isaac Cloud household, 1850 U.S. census, Murray County, Georgia, stamped p. 150B, dwelling 40.

46. Jo Ann Garren Finnell, *The Resting Places: Cemeteries of Polk County, Tennessee* (no place, privately printed, no date), 460.

47. Ibid.

48. Polk County, Tennessee, 1861 tax list, microfilm 7, Monroe to Robertson Counties, Tennessee State Library and Archives, Nashville, Tennessee.

49. James M. Cloud household, 1850 U.S. census, Murray County, Georgia, stamped

p. 150B, dwelling 44. His father Isaac lived in dwelling 40.

50. Byron and Barbara Sistler, *Early East Tennessee Marriages, Volume 1 Grooms* (Nashville: Byron Sistler & Associates, Inc., 1987), 385. Her name is Usler Cloud in this document. Also 1850 U.S. census, Polk County, Tennessee, Civil District 5, stamped p. 238, dwelling 630, family 636. Her name is spelled in the census as pronounced, Eusley.

51. Isaac Cloud household, 1850 U.S. census, Murray County, Georgia, stamped p. 150B, dwelling 40.

52. Polk County, Tennessee, 1861 tax list, microfilm 7, Monroe to Robertson Counties, Tennessee State Library and Archives, Nashville, Tennessee.

53. James M. Cloud household, 1850 U.S. census, Murray County, Georgia, stamped p. 150B, dwelling 44. His father Isaac lived in dwelling 40.

54. *Cloud Family of Scott County, Mississippi*, 2. Copy held in 2011 by Bob McDill (Nashville, Tennessee).

55. Murray County, Georgia, marriage bond, copy of original held in 2011 by Bob McDill (Nashville, Tennessee).

56. WPA Polk County, Tennessee, Court Minutes 1844–1847, 70, referencing original minutes, 204.

57. James M. Cloud household, 1850 U.S. census, Murray County, Georgia, stamped p. 150B, dwelling 44.

58. James Cloud household, 1860 U.S. census, Polk County, Tennessee, 181–452.

59. Polk County, Tennessee, 1861 tax list, microfilm 7, Monroe to Robertson Counties, Tennessee State Library and Archives, Nashville, Tennessee.

60. *Cloud Family of Scott County, Mississippi*, 2. Copy held in 2011 by Bob McDill (Nashville, Tennessee).

61. Ibid., 17. All information on James Madison Cloud's children is from this publication.

62. Obituary notice, *Mississippi Baptist*, unknown date (1903); copy held in 2010 by Bob McDill (Nashville, Tennessee).

63. James M. Cloud household, 1850 U.S. census, Murray County, Georgia, stamped p. 150B, dwelling 44.

64. Obituary notice, *Mississippi Baptist*, unknown date (1903); copy held in 2011 by Bob McDill (Nashville, Tennessee).

65. Mrs. M. L. Cloud, Tennessee Confederate pension application dated 18 August 1921.

66. Scott County, Mississippi, Record Book 1:100.

67. Ibid.

68. James Cloud household, 1860 U.S. census, Polk County, Tennessee, 181–452.

69. M. L. Cloud military muster rolls, Co. A, 59 Tenn. Mtd. Inf., Tennessee State Library and Archives, Nashville, Tennessee.

70. *Tennesseans in the Civil War, part 1* (Nashville, Tennessee: Civil War Centennial Commission, 1964), 299.

71. Raymond Cloud Hunt, *Ancestors and Descendants of Marquis De Lafayette Cloud and Henrietta Virginia Petty* (McAllen, Texas: no publisher, 1987).

72. William Lovelace Foster, *Vicksburg: Southern City Under Siege* (New Orleans, Louisiana: privately published, 1995), 69.

73. Dunbar Rowland, *Military History of Mississippi* (Spartanburg, South Carolina:

The Ancestors and Descendants of Robert Nathaniel McDill

published unknown, 1978), 322.

74. Foster, 59.

75. Marquis Cloud parole, copy held in 2011 by Bob McDill, Nashville, Tennessee.

76. Hunt, *Ancestors and Descendants of Marquis De Lafayette Cloud and Henrietta Virginia Petty.*

77. *Tennesseans in the Civil War, part 1*, 299.

78. Hunt, 2B.

79. Hunt, *Ancestors and Descendants of Marquis De Lafayette Cloud and Henrietta Virginia Petty.*

80. As told to Bob McDill.

81. Obituary notice, Mississippi Baptist, unknown date (1903), copy held in 2011 by Bob McDill (Nashville, Tennessee).

82. Scott County, Mississippi, Record Book 1:100.

83. *Cloud Family of Scott County, Mississippi*, 9.

84. Ibid.

85. Hunt, 4B.

86. Marcus Cloud household, 1880 U.S. census, Scott County, Mississippi, District 5, stamped p. 101, dwelling 70, family 75.

87. Marcus L. Cloud household, 1900 U.S. census, Scott County, Mississippi, Beat 5, dwelling 169 and family 173.

88. Christiana Petty household, John W. Petty household and Robert McDill household, 1900 U.S. census, Scott County, Mississippi, Beat 5, dwelling 167 and family 171, 166– 170 and 165–169 respectively.

89. Obituary notice, Mississippi Baptist, unknown date (1903); copy held in 2011 by Bob McDill (Nashville, Tennessee).

90. Mrs. M. L. Cloud, Tennessee Confederate pension application dated 18 August 1921.

91. Ibid.

92. Hunt, 4B.

93. Ibid.

94. There is some confusion about "Dell" Cloud McDill's name. Some sources call her Lidia or Lydia. However she is listed as Lida in both the 1900 and 1920 Mississippi censuses. In the 1880 census, she is simply "Dell." Her name is not legible in the 1910 census. These original documents were available for viewing on ancestry.com. On her marriage record, dated 18 Jan. 1898, she is Adella Cloud. So I am assuming her name was Lida Adella. Information from the marriage record was accessed on ancestry.com, which was taken from Mississippi Marriages 1776–1935, Provo, Utah, USA. However, in this case, I was not able to view the original document.

Part 5

1. *Cloud Family of Scott County, Mississippi.* Also Henry M. Pettus, The Pettuses of Corn Hill Plantation, Mecklenburg County, Virginia, and Their Ancestors and Descendants (South Hill, Virginia: privately published, 1966). Also Alice Amis Hodges, Ancestry and Descendants of Dr, John Wright Petty of Madison Co., Ala. (Pendleton, S.C.: privately published, 1966).

2. Alice Amis Hodges, *Ancestry and Descendants of Dr, John Wright Petty of Madison Co., Ala.* (Pendleton, S.C.: privately published, 1966), 37.

3. Pettus, *The Pettuses of Corn Hill Plantation*, Mecklenburg County, Virginia, and

Their Ancestors and Descendants, 7.

4. Warner, *History of Old Rappahannock County, Virginia, 1656–1692*, 164.

5. Ibid.

6. Hodges, 31.

7. Ibid.

8. William Montgomery Sweeny, *Wills of Rappahannock County, Virginia, 1656–1692* (Lynchburg, Virginia: J. P. Bell Co., 1947), 157.

9. Ibid.

10. Warner, *History of Old Rappahannock County, Virginia*, 165 –1692. This record indicates that she was "about" to marry him, not that she actually did so.

11. Sweeny, Wills of Rappahannock County, Virginia, 1656–1692, page 157 states his name as Fugett whereas *Cloud Family of Scott County, Mississippi*, page 23 says his surname was Ferguson.

12. Sweeny, *Wills of Rappahannock County, Virginia, 1656–1692*, 33.

13. John Frederick Dorman, *Essex County, Virginia, Records 1717–1722* (Washington, DC: privately printed, 1959), 62–63.

14. Ibid.

15. *Cloud Family of Scott County, Mississippi*, 22.

16. Ibid.

17. Ulysses P. Joyner, *The First Settlers of Orange County, Virginia* (Baltimore: Gateway Press, 1987), 160. His father Thomas Petty is believed to have died in Orange County in 1720.

18. John Frederick Dorman, *Orange County, Virginia, Will Book 2 1744–1778* (Washington, DC: privately published, 1961), 31.

19. John Frederick Dorman, *Orange County, Virginia, Deed Books 1 and 2* (Washington, DC: privately published, 1961), 10.

20. John Frederick Dorman, *Orange County, Virginia, Deed Books 5, 6, 7, and 8* (Washington, DC: privately published, 1971), 21.

21. *Cloud Family of Scott County, Mississippi*, 22.

22. Ibid.

23. Dorman, *Orange County, Virginia, Deed Books 1 and 2*, 10.

24. Dorman, *Orange County, Virginia, Deed Books 5, 6, 7, and 8*, 21.

25. Ibid., 24.

26. *Cloud Family of Scott County*, Mississippi, p. 22.

27. Ibid.

28. *DAR Patriot Index, Centennial Edition* (Washington, DC: National Society of the Daughters of the America Revolution, 1994), 2293.

29. Elizabeth Prather Ellsberry, *Will Records of Clark County, Kentucky* (Chillicothe, Missouri: privately published, no date), 9. Also *Cloud Family of Scott County, Mississippi*, 22.

30. Hodges, 22.

31. Dorothy Scott Johnson, *Cemeteries of Madison County, Alabama Vol. II* (Huntsville, Alabama: Johnson Historical Publications, 1978), 234.

32. *Cloud Family of Scott County, Mississippi*, 21.

33. Johnson, *Cemeteries of Madison County, Alabama Vol. II*, 234.

34. *Cloud Family of Scott County, Mississippi*, 21.

35. Ibid.

36. Ibid.

37. Johnson, *Cemeteries of Madison County, Alabama Vol. II*, 234.

38. Ibid.
39. *DAR Patriot Index, Centennial Edition*, 2293.
40. Johnson, *Cemeteries of Madison County, Alabama Vol. II*, 234. Also *Cloud Family of Scott County, Mississippi*, 21.
41. Johnson, *Cemeteries of Madison County, Alabama Vol. II*, 234.
42. William Petty, Revolutionary pension S17016, National Archives, Washington, DC.
43. *Cloud Family of Scott County, Mississippi*, 21.
44. Johnson, *Cemeteries of Madison County, Alabama Vol. II*, 234.
45. Ibid., 97.
46. Hodges, 7.
47. Johnson, *Cemeteries of Madison County, Alabama Vol. II*, 97.
48. Johnson, *Cemeteries of Madison County, Alabama Vol. II*, 97.
49. Wicht Brewer household, 1850 U.S. census, Scott County, Mississippi, stamped p. 258, dwelling and family 11. Marriage date estimated from birth of first children.
50. Christiana Petty household, 1860 U.S. census, Scott County, Mississippi, District 5, p. 18, dwelling and family 109.
51. Hunt, 4C.
52. John W. Petty household, 1850 U.S. census, Scott County, Mississippi, stamped p. 258, dwelling and family 13.
53. Christiana Petty household, 1860 U.S. census, Scott County, Mississippi, District 5, p. 18, dwelling and family 109.
54. Christiana Petty household, 1880 U.S. census, Scott County, Mississippi, District 5, stamped p. 101, dwelling 71, family 76.
55. 55 Christiana Petty household, 1900 U.S. census, Scott County, Mississippi, Beat 5, stamped p. 145, dwelling 167, household 171.

Index of Names

A

Adams, Captain Samuel 74
Anderson, Ada Eugenia McDill 110
Anderson, John 126
Anderson, Martha "Mattie" 93
Anderson, William C. Dr. 110
Andrews, Henrietta Virginia (Petty) 144, 146
Arthur, King 18, 22

B

Balliol, John 33
Bardon, Jonathan 63, 173
Barrow, G. S. 30
Bayless, Abigail 160
Bell, Alexander Graham 95
Bell, Robert 42, 172
Bishop, Joshua E. 93
Black, George F. 13, 171
Boswell, James 49
Boyd, William 77
Brena, Jno. 70
Brewer, Christiana 162, 163, 166
Brewer, Flora (McPherson) 163
Brewer, Luvenia 161
Brewer, Wyche 163
Brittace, John 87
Brooke, Daphne 18, 23, 28, 171
Broussard, Dorothy 97, 116, 121
Brown, S. 68
Bruce, Robert 38
Bryan, Cynthia 160
Burns, Mary Jane McDill 108

Burns, William Wesley 93

C

F

Farrell, Hubbard 126
Fergus MacDowall 171
Ferguson, General Patrick 75
Fischer, David H. 51, 71
Flowers, John W., Jr. 139
Foster, William Lovelace 145, 185
Frost, Robert 72, 174
Froude, J. A. 52
Fry, Fiona 20, 27, 30, 31, 171
Fry, Peter 20, 27, 30, 31, 171
Fugett, Dorothy (Pettit) 151
Fugett, James 151

G

Gaines, James 137
Gaines, Joseph 137
Gaines, Thomas 151
Galleran, Sir 22
Gallet, Ann 96
Garret, Richard 128
Garrett, Frances "Fanny" (Callaham) 128
Garrett, William 128
Garton, Catherine 153
Garton, John 153
Gleane, Mary 149
Glover, Richard 150
Gordon, Jean Delores 97

H

Hadrian, Emperor 20
Harbin, Ann 155
Harris, Anna 161
Harrison, Diane Martin 159
Harris, Sarah 161
Heath, Henry Brigadier General 144
Henderson, John 138

Logue, Rev. John 68

M

MacAlpin, Kenneth 26
Macdougall, John 33
Macdowall, David 15
Macdowall, Dugald 33
MacDowall, Fergus 15, 35, 57
MacDowall, John 35
MacDowall, Thomas 35
MacDowall, Uchtred 35
Macduyl, Gilbert 36
MacLean, Fitzroy 29
Madison, James 144
Mallett, Joyce (Callaham) 128
Mallett, Sterling 128
Malone, William 125
Martingale, Richard 150
Martin, Major General William T. 145
Martin, William Rev. 66
May, Oneida 108
McCauley, Ruby Lee 97
McClure, James 81
McCormick, Cyrus 80
McDill, Ada Eugenia 93, 110
McDill, Allie Estelle (Hunt) 93
McDill, Alpha Brucie (Pace) 93
McDill, Amanda 81, 84
McDill, Andrew 36
McDill, Ann 83, 85, 104
McDill, Ann (Gallet) 96
McDill, Annie Idelia (Edwards) 93
McDill, Brucie (Aunt Brucie) 92
McDill, Dan 5
McDill, Dorothy (Broussard) 97, 116, 121
McDill, Ed (Uncle Ed) 92
McDill, Edward Wilder 93, 106

McDill, Elizabeth Ann 83

McDill, Flora E. 83, 84

McDill, Georgia Ann (Sprewell) 83, 176

McDill, Georgianna 84

McDill, Guy Vernon 97, 114, 119, 180

McDill, Hattie (Wall) 94, 96, 170

McDill, Hugh 64

McDill, Isabella Jane 84

McDill, James 78, 83, 91, 176, 177

McDill, Janet (Leslie) 63

McDill, Jean Delores (Gordon) 97

McDill, John A. 83

McDill, John (Bud) 84, 107, 108

McDill, John (follower of the Earl of Cassilis) 36

McDill, John (nephew of Nathaniel Sr.) 74, 77

McDill, John (Old John) 64, 65, 95, 206

McDill, John William 93

McDill, Joseph Alexander 93, 109

McDilll, Ellen 84

McDill, Lidia Adella "Dell" (Cloud). *See* Cloud, Lida Adella "Dell"

McDill, Louise 5, 8

McDill, Marcus Alfred 97, 114

McDill, Margaret (Chestnut) 64, 73

McDill, Margaret Nazarene 93, 106

McDill, Margaret "Peggy" 64

McDill, Martha "Mattie" (Anderson). *See* Anderson, Martha "Mattie"

McDill, Mary 78, 107

McDill, Mary Chestnut 68

MCDill, Mary E. (Dawson) 83

McDill, Mary Jane 93, 108

McDill, Michael 36

McDill, Mollie (Dear). *See* Dear, Mollie

McDill, Nathaniel 64, 65, 67, 70, 74, 76, 77, 79, 83, 173, 175, 176, 177

McDill, Nathaniel Jr. 79, 80, 82, 104

McDill, Nathaniel Logan 81, 83, 84, 86, 91

McDill, Norman Cloud 114, 180

Moore, Francis 155
Moore, Harbin 155
Moore, Robert 81
Morgan, Elizabeth 160
Morgan, John Hunt 145
Morris, Eleanor 150
Morris, George 150
Morris, Katherine 150
Morse, Samuel F. B. 80
Moss, Warren 142

N

Neblett, Sterling 128
Nesbit, Jane 160
Nobles, Jesse 86
Nobles, Nancy 86
Norris, Margaret 162

O

Ogletree, Captain R. D. 89

P

Pace, Alpha Brucie 93
Patrick, B. B. 87
Pedan, James 65, 77
Pedan, John 64, 68, 73, 174
Pedan, Margaret (McDill) "Peggy". *See* McDill, Margaret "Peggy"
Penn, William 135
Pettit, Dorothy 151
Pettit, Katherine (Morris). *See* Morris, Katherine
Pettit, Thomas 150, 151, 152
Pettus, Cecily (King). *See* King, Cecily
Pettus, Henry 149, 203
Pettus, Mary (Gleane). *See* Gleane, Mary
Pettus, Thomas 149, 150
Pettus, William 149
Petty, Abigail (Bayless). *See* Bayless, Abigail

Petty, Albert Gallatin 161, 163

Petty, Amelia 160

Petty, Ann 156

Petty, Anna (Harris). *See* Harris, Anna

Petty, Ann Eliza 162

Petty, Benjamin 152

Petty, Benjamin Franklin 160

Petty, Catherine (Garton). *See* Garton, Catherine

Petty, Christiana (Brewer). *See* Brewer, Christiana

Petty, Christopher 153

Petty, Cornelia 162

Petty, Cynthia (Bryan). *See* Bryan, Cynthia

Petty, Daniel Boone 162

Petty, Daniel Harrison 160

Petty, Dewitt Cinton 161

Petty, Diane Martin (Harrison). *See* Harrison, Diane Martin

Petty, Eli Williams 159

Petty, Elizabeth (Moore). *See* Moore, Elizabeth

Petty, Elizabeth (Morgan). *See* Morgan, Elizabeth

Petty, Emma (Wall) 164

Petty, Flora Ann 164

Petty, Francis Moore 155

Petty, George 152, 154

Petty, Hannah 157

Petty, Henrietta Virginia 163, 170, 183, 185, 203

Petty, James 153, 158

Petty, James William 160

Petty, Jane (Nesbit). *See* Nesbit, Jane

Petty, John 153, 157

Petty, John W. 146, 186, 188

Petty, John William 164

Petty, John Wright 161, 186, 203

Petty, Lazarus 159

Petty, Lettis 157

Petty, Lovey 156

Petty, Lucretia "Lucy" (Wright) 159, 161, 162

Petty, Luvenia (Brewer). *See* Brewer, Luvenia

Petty, Margaret (Norris). *See* Norris, Margaret

Petty, Martha 154

Petty, Mary 152, 154

Petty, Mary (Millsap). *See* Millsap, Mary

Petty, Nancy 159, 162

Petty, Newton Eli 162

Petty, Rachel 152, 157

Petty, Rachel (Wilson) 152

Petty, Randell 157

Petty, Rebecca (Shackleford) 159

Petty, Rebecca (Simms) 153

Petty, Richard P. 162

Petty, Sally 160

Petty, Sarah 158

Petty, Sarah A. 162

Petty, Theophilus 153, 155

Petty, Thomas 153, 158

Petty, Thomas Jr. 155

Petty, Thomas Merce 160

Petty, William 153, 155, 156, 157

Petty, William Eli 157, 159

Petty, William Howard 162

Petty, William Thornton 160

Petty, William W. 161

Petty, William Wright "Albert" 164

Petty, Zachariah 157, 159

Pittman, M.L.D. 87

Prebble, John 32, 39, 172

Prichard, Elizabeth Ann (McDill). *See* McDill, Elizabeth Ann

Prichard, Jonathan 83

R

Raleigh, Walter Sir 45

Randolph, Thomas 33

Ransom, Robert Major General 145

Reeves, Robert 126

Reynold, A. W. Colonel 144

Pedigree Charts

The following pedigree charts chronicle the ancestries of Robert Nathaniel McDill and Lida Adella Cloud McDill. The sources for some of the earliest names, dates, and connections are not cited in this book. They are taken from publications and websites that did not name original sources. In some cases, there are conflicting versions of these early lineages. Some may have been compiled from family records unavailable to researchers. A few may be unreliable. As others have done, I have compiled a "consensus" of these accounts of family ancestral lines, using the names and connections most agreed upon in the resources available to me. Among those publications and web sites are:

1. Alice Amis Hodges, *Ancestry and Descendents of Dr. John Wright Petty of Madison Co., Ala.* (Pendleton South Carolina: privately published, June 1978).

2. Charles Arthur Hoppin, *The Washington-Wright Connection and Some Descendents of Major Francis and Anne (Washington) Wright* (Tyler's Quarterly Historical and Genealogical Magazine, January, 1923, Vol. IV,

No. 3).

3. Raymond Cloud Hunt, *Ancestors and Descendents of Marquis de Lafayette Cloud and Henrietta Virginia Petty* (McAllen Texas: Privately Published, 1987).

4. Henry Pettus, *The Pettuses of Corn Hill Plantation, Mecklenburg Co., Virginia* (Privately Printed, 1966).

5. Gary Boyd Roberts, *Ancestors of American Presidents* (Boston: New England Historical Society, 1995).

6. Gerald M. Petty, *Petty, Wright, Riley and Related Families* (Ann Arbor, Michigan: Edwards Brothers, 1973).

7. Margaret Ordrowaz-Sypniewska, B.F.A., "The Lineage of George Washington"Angelfire.com, Polish History, Heraldry and Genealogy, 2006 (5/2012).

8. "John L. Brewer Genealogy,"
geni.com/people/John-Brewer/6000000000574459520 (6/2012).

9. WikiTree, "Major Francis Wright,"
wikitree.com/genealogy/Wright-Family-Tree-745 (6/2012).

Pedigree Chart

Completed Ordinances:
B Baptized
E Endowed
P Sealed to parents
S Sealed to spouse
C Children's ordinances

8 Nathaniel McDill II   2
B: 1775
P: South Carolina
M 1814
P: South Carolina
D: 20 Jan 1857
P: Tallapoosa Co. AL

4 Thomas Alexander McDill
B: 26 Nov 1826
P: South Carolina
M 15 Dec 1857
P: Chambers Co. Ala
D: 23 Sep 1909
P: Newton Co. Miss.

9 Ann Leslie (Logan?)
B: 1795
P: S.C.
D: 24 May 1872
P: Elmore Co. Ala.

2 Robert Nathaniel McDill
B: 8 Aug 1867
P: Scott Co., Mississippi
M 18 Jan 1898
P: Scott Co., Mississippi
D: 25 Aug 1960
P: Union, Mississippi

10 Samuel W. Callaham   3
B: 1811
P: Edgefield District, South Carolina
M
P:
D: Bef 1900
P: Newton Co., Mississippi

5 Sarah Elizabeth Callahan
P: South Carolina
P: Alabama
D: 25 Sep 1933
P: Newton Co., Mississippi

11 Caroline
B: 1822
P: South Carolina
D:
P:

1 Guy Vernon McDill
B: 7 May 1910
P: Newton Co., Mississippi
M: 14 Nov 1937
P: Bmt., Texas
D: 18 Dec 1973
P: Beaumont, Texas

12 James Madison Cloud   4
B: Abt 1817
P: Tennessee
M 20 Mar 1838
P: Murray Co. Georgia
D: 1868
P: Rapides Parish, Louisiana

6 Marquis Lafayette Cloud
B: 22 Dec 1842
P: Georgia
M 30 Apr 1874
P: Scott Co., Miss.
D: 14 Aug 1903
P: Scott Co., Miss

Ruby Lee McCauley
(Spouse of no. 1)

13 Margaret "Peggy" King
B:
P:
D: 1882
P: Scott Co. Miss

3 Lida Adella Cloud
B: 24 Jun 1877
P: Scott Co., Miss
D: 19 Jun 1928
P: Scott Co., Miss.

14 John Wright Petty II   5
B: 12 Nov 1824
P: Madison County, Ala.
M
P:
D: 27 Mar 1858
P: Scott Co., Miss.

7 Henrietta Virginia Petty
B: 28 Jun 1848
P: Scott Co., Miss.
D: 13 Dec 1925
P: LaFeria, Texas

15 Christiana Brewer   6
B: 14 Mar 1827
P: Butler Co.,, Alabama
D: 14 Jun 1909
P: Scott Co., Miss.

No. 1 on this chart is the same as no. 8 on chart no. 1

Completed Ordinances:
B Baptized
E Endowed
P Sealed to parents
S Sealed to spouse
C Children's ordinances

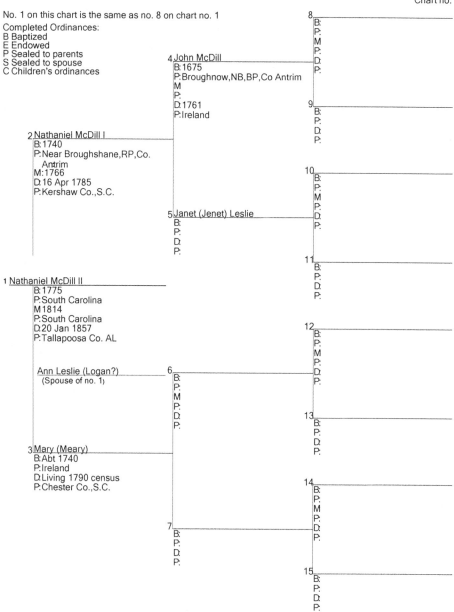

8
B:
P:
M
P:
D:
P:

4 John McDill
B: 1675
P: Broughnow,NB,BP,Co Antrim
M
P:
D: 1761
P: Ireland

9
B:
P:
D:
P:

2 Nathaniel McDill I
B: 1740
P: Near Broughshane,RP,Co.
  Antrim
M: 1766
D: 16 Apr 1785
P: Kershaw Co.,S.C.

10
B:
P:
M
P:
D:
P:

5 Janet (Jenet) Leslie
B:
P:
D:
P:

11
B:
P:
D:
P:

1 Nathaniel McDill II
B: 1775
P: South Carolina
M 1814
P: South Carolina
D: 20 Jan 1857
P: Tallapoosa Co. AL

12
B:
P:
M
P:
D:
P:

Ann Leslie (Logan?)
  (Spouse of no. 1)

6
B:
P:
M
P:
D:
P:

13
B:
P:
D:
P:

3 Mary (Meary)
B: Abt 1740
P: Ireland
D: Living 1790 census
P: Chester Co.,S.C.

14
B:
P:
M
P:
D:
P:

7
B:
P:
D:
P:

15
B:
P:
D:
P:

Bob McDill

No. 1 on this chart is the same as no. 10 on chart no. 1

Completed Ordinances:
B Baptized
E Endowed
P Sealed to parents
S Sealed to spouse
C Children's ordinances

8 Nicholas Callaham
B: Bef. 1693
P: Virginia
M: Before 1719
P:
D: After 1752
P:

4 John Callaham
B: About 1732
P: Surrey Co. Virginia
M
P:
D: Abt 1804
P: Lunenburg Co., Virginia

9 Joyce Weaver   7
B: Bef 1699
P:
D:
P:

2 Morris Callaham
B: 1755/1765
P: Virginia
M
P:
D: 1823
P: Edgefield District, South Carolina

10
B:
P:
M
P:
D:
P:

5
B:
P:
D:
P:

11
B:
P:
D:
P:

1 Samuel W. Callaham
B: 1811
P: Edgefield District, South Carolina
M: About 1837
P:
D: Bef 1900
P: Newton Co., Mississippi

12
B:
P:
M
P:
D:
P:

Caroline
(Spouse of no. 1)

6
B:
P:
M
P:
D:
P:

13
B:
P:
D:
P:

3 Mary
B:
P:
D:
P:

14
B:
P:
M
P:
D:
P:

7
B:
P:
D:
P:

15
B:
P:
D:
P:

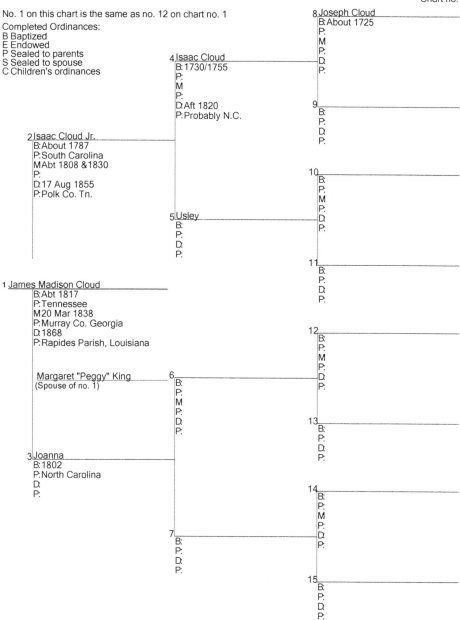

No. 1 on this chart is the same as no. 12 on chart no. 1

Completed Ordinances:
B Baptized
E Endowed
P Sealed to parents
S Sealed to spouse
C Children's ordinances

8 Joseph Cloud
B:About 1725
P:
M
P:
D:
P:

4 Isaac Cloud
B:1730/1755
P:
M
P:
D:Aft 1820
P:Probably N.C.

9
B:
P:
D:
P:

2 Isaac Cloud Jr.
B:About 1787
P:South Carolina
MAbt 1808 &1830
P:
D:17 Aug 1855
P:Polk Co. Tn.

10
B:
P:
M
P:
D:
P:

5 Usley
B:
P:
D:
P:

11
B:
P:
D:
P:

1 James Madison Cloud
B:Abt 1817
P:Tennessee
M20 Mar 1838
P:Murray Co. Georgia
D:1868
P:Rapides Parish, Louisiana

12
B:
P:
M
P:
D:
P:

Margaret "Peggy" King
(Spouse of no. 1)

6
B:
P:
M
P:
D:
P:

13
B:
P:
D:
P:

3 Joanna
B:1802
P:North Carolina
D:
P:

14
B:
P:
M
P:
D:
P:

7
B:
P:
D:
P:

15
B:
P:
D:
P:

No. 1 on this chart is the same as no. 14 on chart no. 1

Completed Ordinances:
B Baptized
E Endowed
P Sealed to parents
S Sealed to spouse
C Children's ordinances

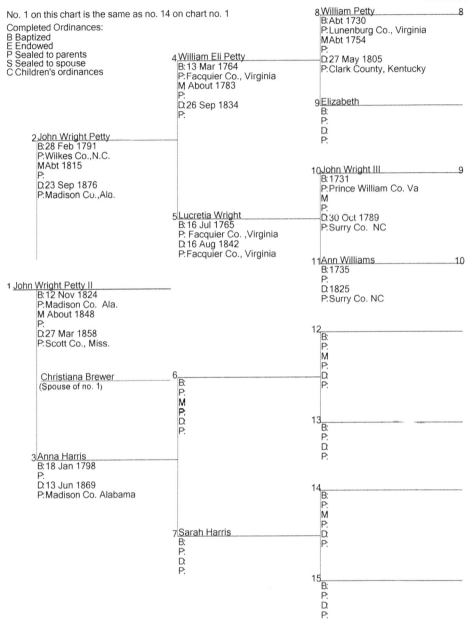

8 William Petty — 8
B: Abt 1730
P: Lunenburg Co., Virginia
M Abt 1754
P:
D: 27 May 1805
P: Clark County, Kentucky

4 William Eli Petty
B: 13 Mar 1764
P: Facquier Co., Virginia
M About 1783
P:
D: 26 Sep 1834
P:

9 Elizabeth
B:
P:
D:
P:

2 John Wright Petty
B: 28 Feb 1791
P: Wilkes Co., N.C.
M Abt 1815
P:
D: 23 Sep 1876
P: Madison Co., Ala.

10 John Wright III — 9
B: 1731
P: Prince William Co. Va
M
P:
D: 30 Oct 1789
P: Surry Co. NC

5 Lucretia Wright
B: 16 Jul 1765
P: Facquier Co., Virginia
D: 16 Aug 1842
P: Facquier Co., Virginia

11 Ann Williams — 10
B: 1735
P:
D: 1825
P: Surry Co. NC

1 John Wright Petty II
B: 12 Nov 1824
P: Madison Co. Ala.
M About 1848
P:
D: 27 Mar 1858
P: Scott Co., Miss.

12
B:
P:
M
P:
D:
P:

Christiana Brewer
(Spouse of no. 1)

6
B:
P:
M
P:
D:
P:

13
B:
P:
D:
P:

3 Anna Harris
B: 18 Jan 1798
P:
D: 13 Jun 1869
P: Madison Co. Alabama

14
B:
P:
M
P:
D:
P:

7 Sarah Harris
B:
P:
D:
P:

15
B:
P:
D:
P:

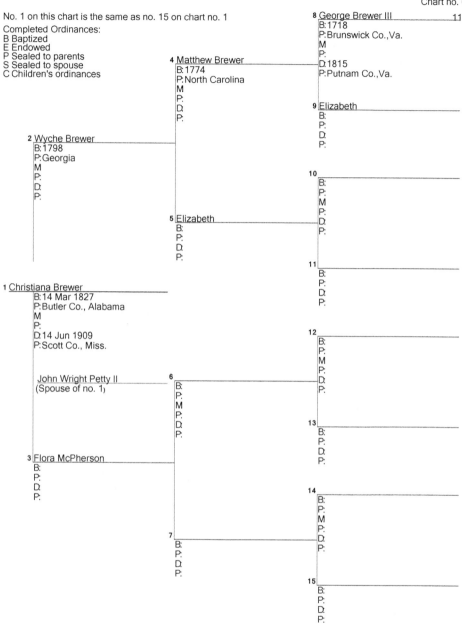

No. 1 on this chart is the same as no. 15 on chart no. 1

Completed Ordinances:
B Baptized
E Endowed
P Sealed to parents
S Sealed to spouse
C Children's ordinances

8 George Brewer III _____ 11
B:1718
P:Brunswick Co.,Va.
M
P:
D:1815
P:Putnam Co.,Va.

4 Matthew Brewer
B:1774
P:North Carolina
M
P:
D:
P:

9 Elizabeth
B:
P:
D:
P:

2 Wyche Brewer
B:1798
P:Georgia
M
P:
D:
P:

10
B:
P:
M
P:
D:
P:

5 Elizabeth
B:
P:
D:
P:

11
B:
P:
D:
P:

1 Christiana Brewer
B:14 Mar 1827
P:Butler Co., Alabama
M
P:
D:14 Jun 1909
P:Scott Co., Miss.

12
B:
P:
M
P:
D:
P:

John Wright Petty II
(Spouse of no. 1)

6
B:
P:
M
P:
D:
P:

13
B:
P:
D:
P:

3 Flora McPherson
B:
P:
D:
P:

14
B:
P:
M
P:
D:
P:

7
B:
P:
D:
P:

15
B:
P:
D:
P:

Bob McDill

211

No. 1 on this chart is the same as no. 9 on chart no. 3

Completed Ordinances:
B Baptized
E Endowed
P Sealed to parents
S Sealed to spouse
C Children's ordinances

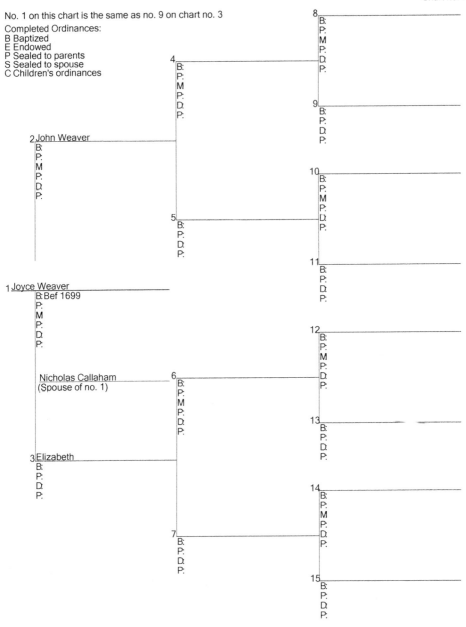

8
B:
P:
M
P:
D:
P:

4
B:
P:
M
P:
D:
P:

9
B:
P:
D:
P:

2 John Weaver
B:
P:
M
P:
D:
P:

10
B:
P:
M
P:
D:
P:

5
B:
P:
D:
P:

11
B:
P:
D:
P:

1 Joyce Weaver
B: Bef 1699
P:
M
P:
D:
P:

12
B:
P:
M
P:
D:
P:

Nicholas Callaham
(Spouse of no. 1)

6
B:
P:
M
P:
D:
P:

13
B:
P:
D:
P:

3 Elizabeth
B:
P:
D:
P:

14
B:
P:
M
P:
D:
P:

7
B:
P:
D:
P:

15
B:
P:
D:
P:

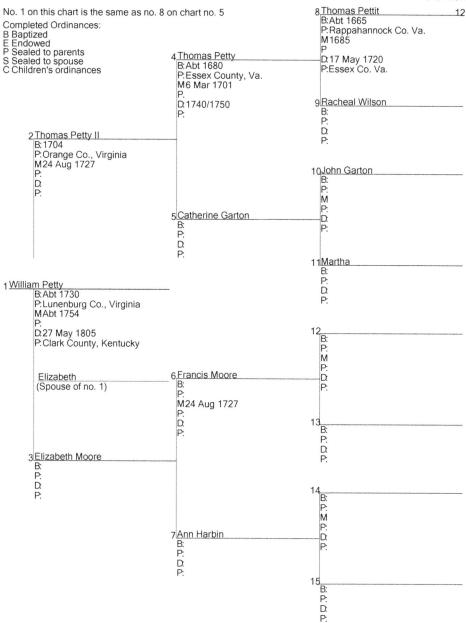

No. 1 on this chart is the same as no. 8 on chart no. 5

Completed Ordinances:
B Baptized
E Endowed
P Sealed to parents
S Sealed to spouse
C Children's ordinances

8 Thomas Pettit   12
B: Abt 1665
P: Rappahannock Co. Va.
M 1685
P
D: 17 May 1720
P: Essex Co. Va.

4 Thomas Petty
B: Abt 1680
P: Essex County, Va.
M 6 Mar 1701
P.
D: 1740/1750
P:

9 Racheal Wilson
B:
P:
D:
P:

2 Thomas Petty II
B: 1704
P: Orange Co., Virginia
M 24 Aug 1727
P:
D:
P:

10 John Garton
B:
P:
M
P:
D:
P:

5 Catherine Garton
B:
P:
D:
P:

11 Martha
B:
P:
D:
P:

1 William Petty
B: Abt 1730
P: Lunenburg Co., Virginia
M Abt 1754
P:
D: 27 May 1805
P: Clark County, Kentucky

12
B:
P:
M
P:
D:
P:

Elizabeth
(Spouse of no. 1)

6 Francis Moore
B:
P:
M 24 Aug 1727
P:
D:
P:

13
B:
P:
D:
P:

3 Elizabeth Moore
B:
P:
D:
P:

14
B:
P:
M
P:
D:
P:

7 Ann Harbin
B:
P:
D:
P:

15
B:
P:
D:
P:

Chart no. 9

No. 1 on this chart is the same as no. 10 on chart no. 5

Completed Ordinances:
B Baptized
E Endowed
P Sealed to parents
S Sealed to spouse
C Children's ordinances

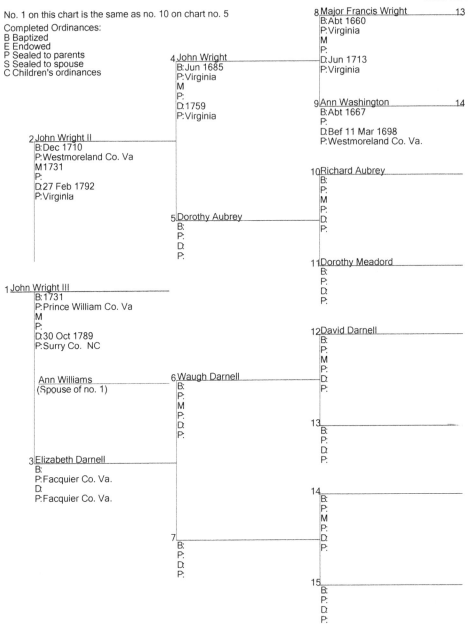

8 Major Francis Wright   13
B: Abt 1660
P: Virginia
M
P:
D: Jun 1713
P: Virginia

4 John Wright
B: Jun 1685
P: Virginia
M
P:
D: 1759
P: Virginia

9 Ann Washington   14
B: Abt 1667
P:
D: Bef 11 Mar 1698
P: Westmoreland Co. Va.

2 John Wright II
B: Dec 1710
P: Westmoreland Co. Va
M 1731
P:
D: 27 Feb 1792
P: Virginla

10 Richard Aubrey
B:
P:
M
P:
D:
P:

5 Dorothy Aubrey
B:
P:
D:
P:

11 Dorothy Meadord
B:
P:
D:
P:

1 John Wright III
B: 1731
P: Prince William Co. Va
M
P:
D: 30 Oct 1789
P: Surry Co. NC

12 David Darnell
B:
P:
M
P:
D:
P:

Ann Williams
(Spouse of no. 1)

6 Waugh Darnell
B:
P:
M
P:
D:
P:

13
B:
P:
D:
P:

3 Elizabeth Darnell
B:
P: Facquier Co. Va.
D:
P: Facquier Co. Va.

14
B:
P:
M
P:
D:
P:

7
B:
P:
D:
P:

15
B:
P:
D:
P:

No. 1 on this chart is the same as no. 11 on chart no. 5

Completed Ordinances:
B Baptized
E Endowed
P Sealed to parents
S Sealed to spouse
C Children's ordinances

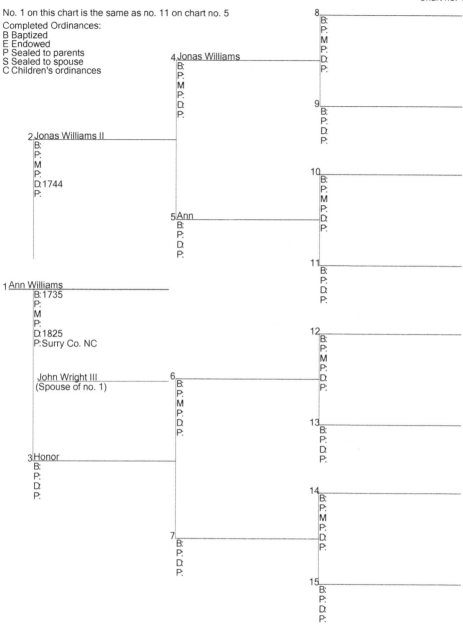

8
B:
P:
M
P:
D:
P:

4 Jonas Williams
B:
P:
M
P:
D:
P:

9
B:
P:
D:
P:

2 Jonas Williams II
B:
P:
M
P:
D:1744
P:

10
B:
P:
M
P:
D:
P:

5 Ann
B:
P:
D:
P:

11
B:
P:
D:
P:

1 Ann Williams
B:1735
P:
M
P:
D:1825
P:Surry Co. NC

12
B:
P:
M
P:
D:
P:

John Wright III
(Spouse of no. 1)

6
B:
P:
M
P:
D:
P:

13
B:
P:
D:
P:

3 Honor
B:
P:
D:
P:

14
B:
P:
M
P:
D:
P:

7
B:
P:
D:
P:

15
B:
P:
D:
P:

Bob McDill

215

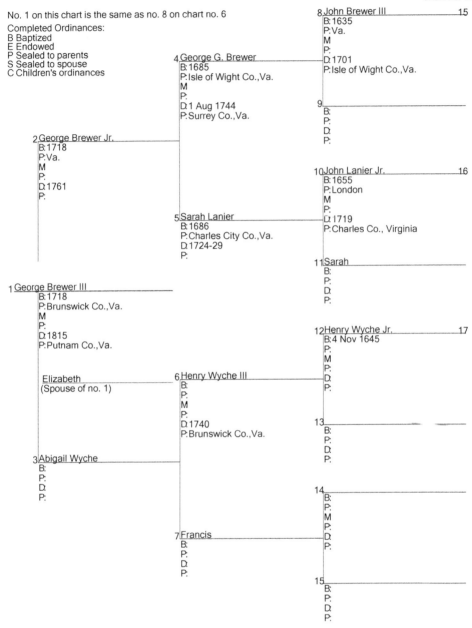

No. 1 on this chart is the same as no. 8 on chart no. 6

Completed Ordinances:
B Baptized
E Endowed
P Sealed to parents
S Sealed to spouse
C Children's ordinances

8 John Brewer III _____ 15
B: 1635
P: Va.
M
P:
D: 1701
P: Isle of Wight Co., Va.

4 George G. Brewer _____
B: 1685
P: Isle of Wight Co., Va.
M
P:
D: 1 Aug 1744
P: Surrey Co., Va.

9 _____
B:
P:
D:
P:

2 George Brewer Jr. _____
B: 1718
P: Va.
M
P:
D: 1761
P:

10 John Lanier Jr. _____ 16
B: 1655
P: London
M
P:
D: 1719
P: Charles Co., Virginia

5 Sarah Lanier _____
B: 1686
P: Charles City Co., Va.
D: 1724-29
P:

11 Sarah _____
B:
P:
D:
P:

1 George Brewer III _____
B: 1718
P: Brunswick Co., Va.
M
P:
D: 1815
P: Putnam Co., Va.

Elizabeth _____
(Spouse of no. 1)

12 Henry Wyche Jr. _____ 17
B: 4 Nov 1645
P:
M
P:
D:
P:

6 Henry Wyche III _____
B:
P:
M
P:
D: 1740
P: Brunswick Co., Va.

13 _____
B:
P:
D:
P:

3 Abigail Wyche _____
B:
P:
D:
P:

14 _____
B:
P:
M
P:
D:
P:

7 Francis _____
B:
P:
D:
P:

15 _____
B:
P:
D:
P:

The Ancestors and Descendants of Robert Nathaniel McDill

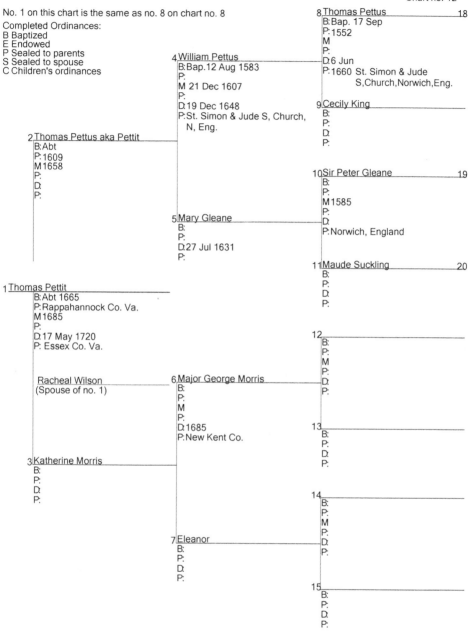

No. 1 on this chart is the same as no. 8 on chart no. 8

Completed Ordinances:
B Baptized
E Endowed
P Sealed to parents
S Sealed to spouse
C Children's ordinances

8 Thomas Pettus   18
B: Bap. 17 Sep
P: 1552
M
P:
D: 6 Jun
P: 1660 St. Simon & Jude
       S, Church, Norwich, Eng.

9 Cecily King
B:
P:
D:
P:

4 William Pettus
B: Bap. 12 Aug 1583
P:
M 21 Dec 1607
P:
D: 19 Dec 1648
P: St. Simon & Jude S, Church,
   N, Eng.

2 Thomas Pettus aka Pettit
B: Abt
P: 1609
M 1658
P:
D:
P:

5 Mary Gleane
B:
P:
D: 27 Jul 1631
P:

10 Sir Peter Gleane   19
B:
P:
M 1585
P:
D:
P: Norwich, England

11 Maude Suckling   20
B:
P:
D:
P:

1 Thomas Pettit
B: Abt 1665
P: Rappahannock Co. Va.
M 1685
P:
D: 17 May 1720
P: Essex Co. Va.

Racheal Wilson
(Spouse of no. 1)

6 Major George Morris
B:
P:
M
P:
D: 1685
P: New Kent Co.

12
B:
P:
M
P:
D:
P:

13
B:
P:
D:
P:

3 Katherine Morris
B:
P:
D:
P:

14
B:
P:
M
P:
D:
P:

7 Eleanor
B:
P:
D:
P:

15
B:
P:
D:
P:

Bob McDill

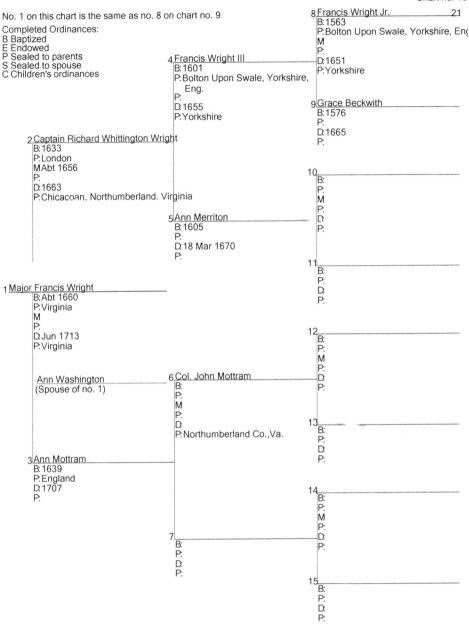

No. 1 on this chart is the same as no. 8 on chart no. 9

Completed Ordinances:
B Baptized
E Endowed
P Sealed to parents
S Sealed to spouse
C Children's ordinances

8 Francis Wright Jr.   21
B: 1563
P: Bolton Upon Swale, Yorkshire, Eng
M
P:
D: 1651
P: Yorkshire

9 Grace Beckwith
B: 1576
P:
D: 1665
P:

4 Francis Wright III
B: 1601
P: Bolton Upon Swale, Yorkshire, Eng.
P:
D: 1655
P: Yorkshire

5 Ann Merriton
B: 1605
P:
D: 18 Mar 1670
P:

2 Captain Richard Whittington Wright
B: 1633
P: London
M Abt 1656
P:
D: 1663
P: Chicacoan, Northumberland. Virginia

10
B:
P:
M
P:
D:
P:

11
B:
P:
D:
P:

1 Major Francis Wright
B: Abt 1660
P: Virginia
M
P:
D: Jun 1713
P: Virginia

Ann Washington
(Spouse of no. 1)

6 Col. John Mottram
B:
P:
M
P:
D:
P: Northumberland Co.,Va.

12
B:
P:
M
P:
D:
P:

13
B:
P:
D:
P:

3 Ann Mottram
B: 1639
P: England
D: 1707
P:

7
B:
P:
D:
P:

14
B:
P:
M
P:
D:
P:

15
B:
P:
D:
P:

No. 1 on this chart is the same as no. 9 on chart no. 9

Completed Ordinances:
B Baptized
E Endowed
P Sealed to parents
S Sealed to spouse
C Children's ordinances

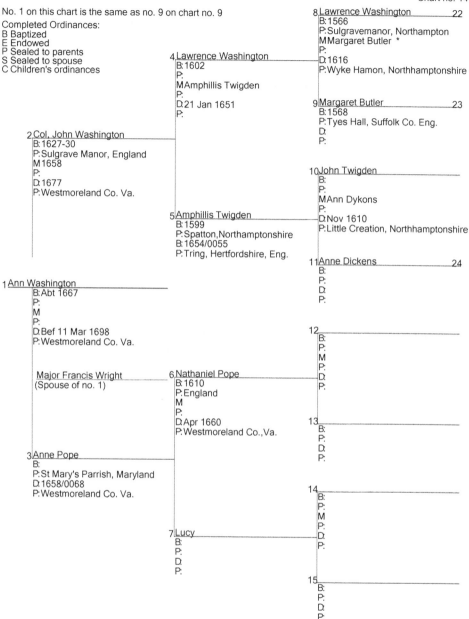

8 Lawrence Washington   22
B: 1566
P: Sulgravemanor, Northampton
M Margaret Butler *
P:
D: 1616
P: Wyke Hamon, Northhamptonshire

4 Lawrence Washington
B: 1602
P:
M Amphillis Twigden
P:
D: 21 Jan 1651
P:

9 Margaret Butler   23
B: 1568
P: Tyes Hall, Suffolk Co. Eng.
D:
P:

2 Col. John Washington
B: 1627-30
P: Sulgrave Manor, England
M 1658
P:
D: 1677
P: Westmoreland Co. Va.

10 John Twigden
B:
P:
M Ann Dykons
P:
D: Nov 1610
P: Little Creation, Northhamptonshire

5 Amphillis Twigden
B: 1599
P: Spatton, Northamptonshire
B: 1654/0055
P: Tring, Hertfordshire, Eng.

11 Anne Dickens   24
B:
P:
D:
P:

1 Ann Washington
B: Abt 1667
P:
M
P:
D: Bef 11 Mar 1698
P: Westmoreland Co. Va.

12
B:
P:
M
P:
D:
P:

Major Francis Wright
(Spouse of no. 1)

6 Nathaniel Pope
B: 1610
P: England
M
P:
D: Apr 1660
P: Westmoreland Co., Va.

13
B:
P:
D:
P:

3 Anne Pope
B:
P: St Mary's Parrish, Maryland
D: 1658/0068
P: Westmoreland Co. Va.

14
B:
P:
M
P:
D:
P:

7 Lucy
B:
P:
D:
P:

15
B:
P:
D:
P:

Bob McDill

219

No. 1 on this chart is the same as no. 8 on chart no. 11

Completed Ordinances:
B Baptized
E Endowed
P Sealed to parents
S Sealed to spouse
C Children's ordinances

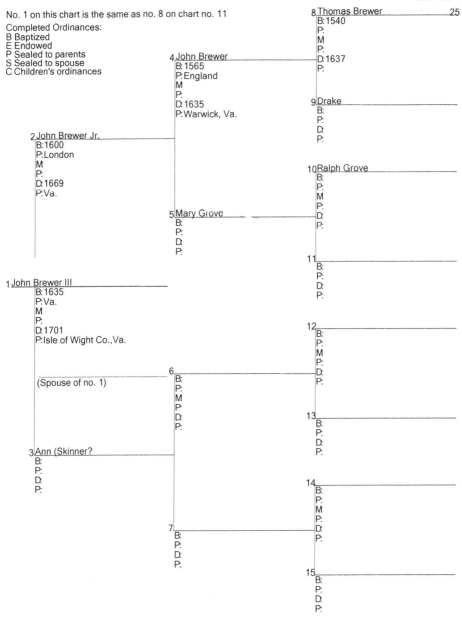

8 Thomas Brewer   25
B: 1540
P:
M
P:
D: 1637
P:

4 John Brewer
B: 1565
P: England
M
P:
D: 1635
P: Warwick, Va.

9 Drake
B:
P:
D:
P:

2 John Brewer Jr.
B: 1600
P: London
M
P:
D: 1669
P: Va.

10 Ralph Grove
B:
P:
M
P:
D:
P:

5 Mary Grove
B:
P:
D:
P:

11
B:
P:
D:
P:

1 John Brewer III
B: 1635
P: Va.
M
P:
D: 1701
P: Isle of Wight Co.,Va.

12
B:
P:
M
P:
D:
P:

(Spouse of no. 1)

6
B:
P:
M
P:
D:
P:

13
B:
P:
D:
P:

3 Ann (Skinner?
B:
P:
D:
P:

14
B:
P:
M
P:
D:
P:

7
B:
P:
D:
P:

15
B:
P:
D:
P:

The Ancestors and Descendants of Robert Nathaniel McDill

No. 1 on this chart is the same as no. 10 on chart no. 11

Completed Ordinances:
B Baptized
E Endowed
P Sealed to parents
S Sealed to spouse
C Children's ordinances

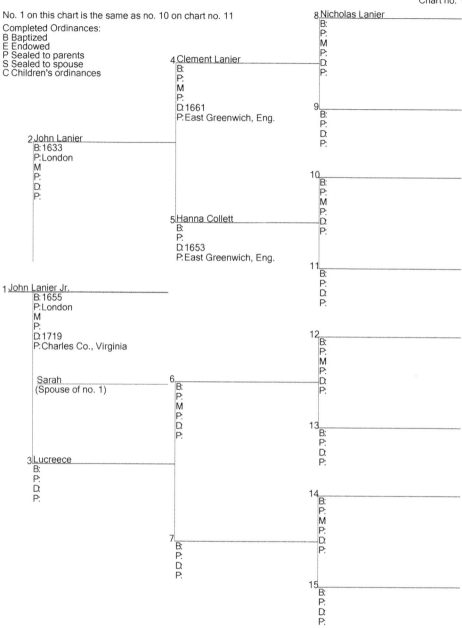

8 Nicholas Lanier
B:
P:
M
P:
D:
P:

4 Clement Lanier
B:
P:
M
P:
D: 1661
P: East Greenwich, Eng.

9
B:
P:
D:
P:

2 John Lanier
B: 1633
P: London
M
P:
D:
P:

10
B:
P:
M
P:
D:
P:

5 Hanna Collett
B:
P:
D: 1653
P: East Greenwich, Eng.

11
B:
P:
D:
P:

1 John Lanier Jr.
B: 1655
P: London
M
P:
D: 1719
P: Charles Co., Virginia

12
B:
P:
M
P:
D:
P:

Sarah
(Spouse of no. 1)

6
B:
P:
M
P:
D:
P:

13
B:
P:
D:
P:

3 Lucreece
B:
P:
D:
P:

14
B:
P:
M
P:
D:
P:

7
B:
P:
D:
P:

15
B:
P:
D:
P:

No. 1 on this chart is the same as no. 12 on chart no. 11

Completed Ordinances:
B Baptized
E Endowed
P Sealed to parents
S Sealed to spouse
C Children's ordinances

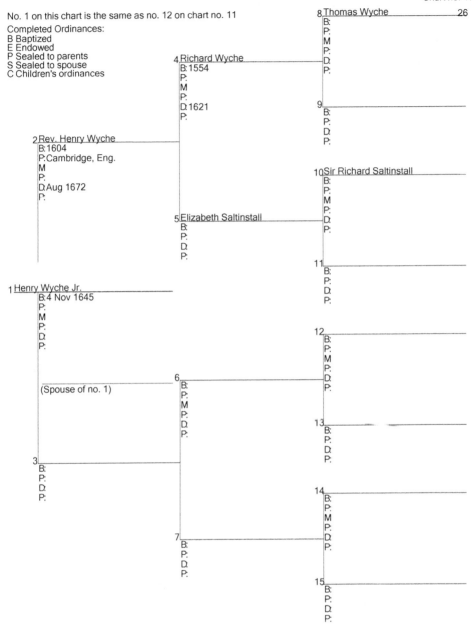

8 Thomas Wyche   26
B:
P:
M
P:
D:
P:

4 Richard Wyche
B: 1554
P:
M
P:
D: 1621
P:

9
B:
P:
D:
P:

2 Rev. Henry Wyche
B: 1604
P: Cambridge, Eng.
M
P:
D: Aug 1672
P:

10 Sir Richard Saltinstall
B:
P:
M
P:
D:
P:

5 Elizabeth Saltinstall
B:
P:
D:
P:

11
B:
P:
D:
P:

1 Henry Wyche Jr.
B: 4 Nov 1645
P:
M
P:
D:
P:

12
B:
P:
M
P:
D:
P:

6
B:
P:
M
P:
D:
P:

(Spouse of no. 1)

13
B:
P:
D:
P:

3
B:
P:
D:
P:

14
B:
P:
M
P:
D:
P:

7
B:
P:
D:
P:

15
B:
P:
D:
P:

No. 1 on this chart is the same as no. 8 on chart no. 12

Completed Ordinances:
B Baptized
E Endowed
P Sealed to parents
S Sealed to spouse
C Children's ordinances

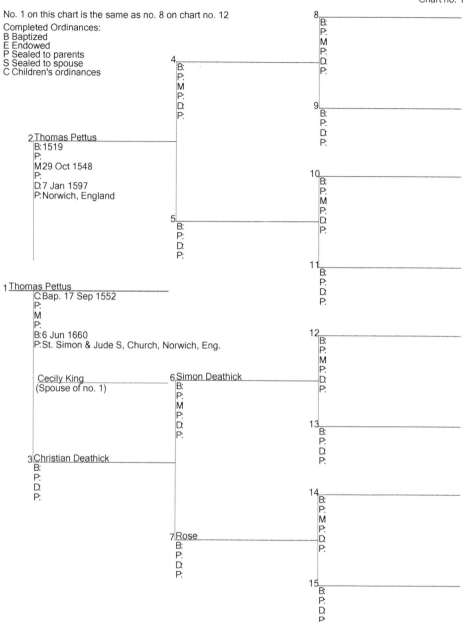

8
B:
P:
M
P:
D:
P:

9
B:
P:
D:
P:

4
B:
P:
M
P:
D:
P:

10
B:
P:
M
P:
D:
P:

2 Thomas Pettus
B: 1519
P:
M 29 Oct 1548
P:
D: 7 Jan 1597
P: Norwich, England

5
B:
P:
D:
P:

11
B:
P:
D:
P:

1 Thomas Pettus
C Bap. 17 Sep 1552
P:
M
P:
B: 6 Jun 1660
P: St. Simon & Jude S, Church, Norwich, Eng.

12
B:
P:
M
P:
D:
P:

Cecily King
(Spouse of no. 1)

6 Simon Deathick
B:
P:
M
P:
D:
P:

13
B:
P:
D:
P:

3 Christian Deathick
B:
P:
D:
P:

14
B:
P:
M
P:
D:
P:

7 Rose
B:
P:
D:
P:

15
B:
P:
D:
P:

No. 1 on this chart is the same as no. 10 on chart no. 12

Completed Ordinances:
B Baptized
E Endowed
P Sealed to parents
S Sealed to spouse
C Children's ordinances

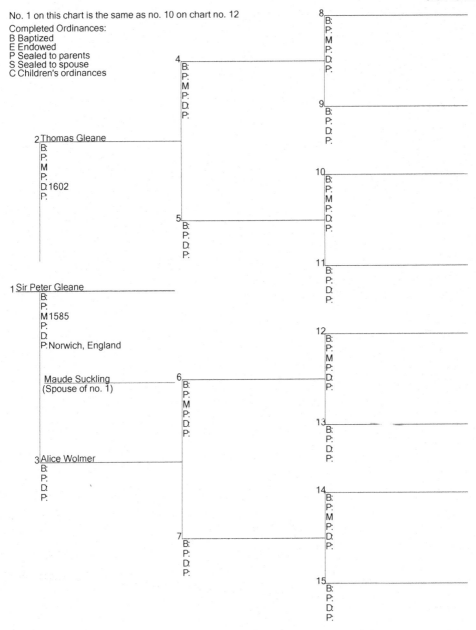

8
B:
P:
M
P:
D:
P:

4
B:
P:
M
P:
D:
P:

9
B:
P:
D:
P:

2 Thomas Gleane
B:
P:
M
P:
D: 1602
P:

10
B:
P:
M
P:
D:
P:

5
B:
P:
D:
P:

11
B:
P:
D:
P:

1 Sir Peter Gleane
B:
P:
M 1585
P:
D:
P: Norwich, England

12
B:
P:
M
P:
D:
P:

Maude Suckling
(Spouse of no. 1)

6
B:
P:
M
P:
D:
P:

13
B:
P:
D:
P:

3 Alice Wolmer
B:
P:
D:
P:

14
B:
P:
M
P:
D:
P:

7
B:
P:
D:
P:

15
B:
P:
D:
P:

The Ancestors and Descendants of Robert Nathaniel McDill

No. 1 on this chart is the same as no. 11 on chart no. 12

Completed Ordinances:
B Baptized
E Endowed
P Sealed to parents
S Sealed to spouse
C Children's ordinances

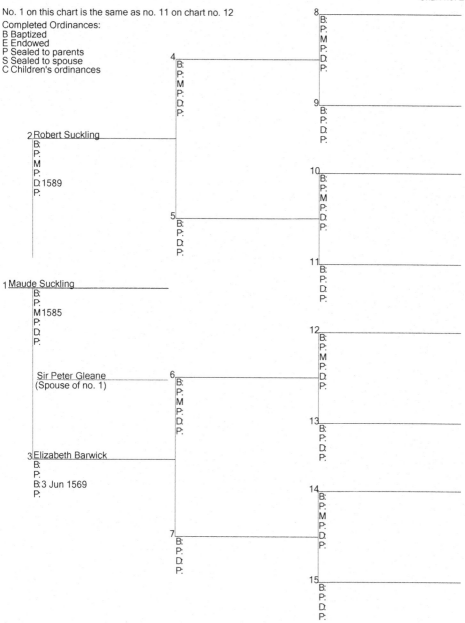

8
B:
P:
M
P:
D:
P:

4
B:
P:
M
P:
D:
P:

9
B:
P:
D:
P:

2 Robert Suckling
B:
P:
M
P:
D: 1589
P:

10
B:
P:
M
P:
D:
P:

5
B:
P:
D:
P:

11
B:
P:
D:
P:

1 Maude Suckling
B:
P:
M 1585
P:
D:
P:

12
B:
P:
M
P:
D:
P:

Sir Peter Gleane
(Spouse of no. 1)

6
B:
P:
M
P:
D:
P:

13
B:
P:
D:
P:

3 Elizabeth Barwick
B:
P:
B: 3 Jun 1569
P:

14
B:
P:
M
P:
D:
P:

7
B:
P:
D:
P:

15
B:
P:
D:
P:

No. 1 on this chart is the same as no. 8 on chart no. 13

Completed Ordinances:
B Baptized
E Endowed
P Sealed to parents
S Sealed to spouse
C Children's ordinances

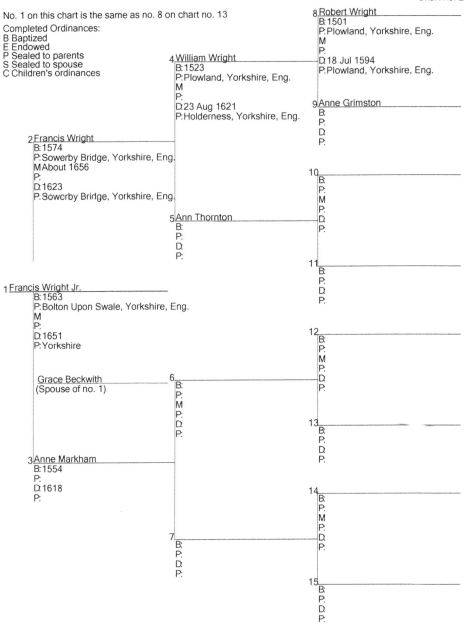

8 Robert Wright
B: 1501
P: Plowland, Yorkshire, Eng.
M
P:
D: 18 Jul 1594
P: Plowland, Yorkshire, Eng.

4 William Wright
B: 1523
P: Plowland, Yorkshire, Eng.
M
P:
D: 23 Aug 1621
P: Holderness, Yorkshire, Eng.

9 Anne Grimston
B:
P:
D:
P:

2 Francis Wright
B: 1574
P: Sowerby Bridge, Yorkshire, Eng.
M About 1656
P:
D: 1623
P: Sowerby Bridge, Yorkshire, Eng.

10
B:
P:
M
P:
D:
P:

5 Ann Thornton
B:
P:
D:
P:

11
B:
P:
D:
P:

1 Francis Wright Jr.
B: 1563
P: Bolton Upon Swale, Yorkshire, Eng.
M
P:
D: 1651
P: Yorkshire

12
B:
P:
M
P:
D:
P:

Grace Beckwith
(Spouse of no. 1)

6
B:
P:
M
P:
D:
P:

13
B:
P:
D:
P:

3 Anne Markham
B: 1554
P:
D: 1618
P:

14
B:
P:
M
P:
D:
P:

7
B:
P:
D:
P:

15
B:
P:
D:
P:

The Ancestors and Descendants of Robert Nathaniel McDill

No. 1 on this chart is the same as no. 8 on chart no. 14

Completed Ordinances:
B Baptized
E Endowed
P Sealed to parents
S Sealed to spouse
C Children's ordinances

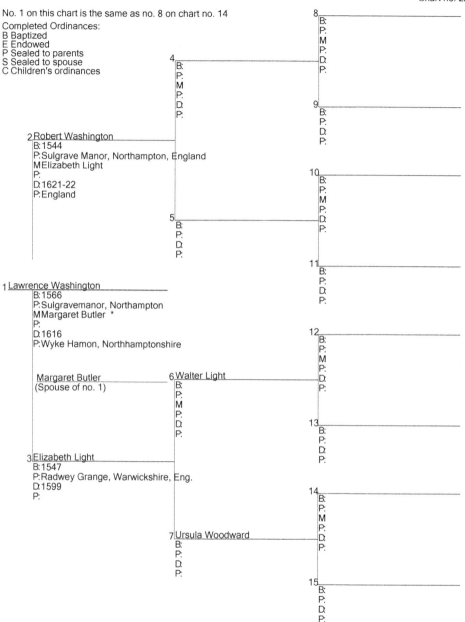

8
B:
P:
M
P:
D:
P:

4
B:
P:
M
P:
D:
P:

9
B:
P:
D:
P:

2 Robert Washington
B: 1544
P: Sulgrave Manor, Northampton, England
M Elizabeth Light
P:
D: 1621-22
P: England

10
B:
P:
M
P:
D:
P:

5
B:
P:
D:
P:

11
B:
P:
D:
P:

1 Lawrence Washington
B: 1566
P: Sulgravemanor, Northampton
M Margaret Butler *
P:
D: 1616
P: Wyke Hamon, Northhamptonshire

12
B:
P:
M
P:
D:
P:

Margaret Butler
(Spouse of no. 1)

6 Walter Light
B:
P:
M
P:
D:
P:

13
B:
P:
D:
P:

3 Elizabeth Light
B: 1547
P: Radwey Grange, Warwickshire, Eng.
D: 1599
P:

14
B:
P:
M
P:
D:
P:

7 Ursula Woodward
B:
P:
D:
P:

15
B:
P:
D:
P:

No. 1 on this chart is the same as no. 9 on chart no. 14

Completed Ordinances:
B Baptized
E Endowed
P Sealed to parents
S Sealed to spouse
C Children's ordinances

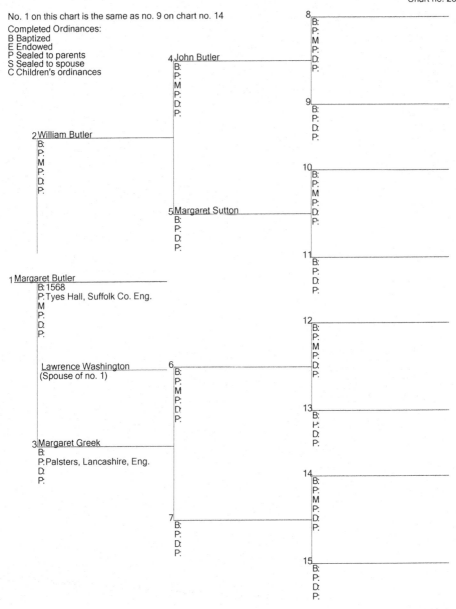

8
B:
P:
M
P:
D:
P:

4 John Butler
B:
P:
M
P:
D:
P:

9
B:
P:
D:
P:

2 William Butler
B:
P:
M
P:
D:
P:

10
B:
P:
M
P:
D:
P:

5 Margaret Sutton
B:
P:
D:
P:

11
B:
P:
D:
P:

1 Margaret Butler
B: 1568
P: Tyes Hall, Suffolk Co. Eng.
M
P:
D:
P:

12
B:
P:
M
P:
D:
P:

Lawrence Washington
(Spouse of no. 1)

6
B:
P:
M
P:
D:
P:

13
B:
P:
D:
P:

3 Margaret Greek
B:
P: Palsters, Lancashire, Eng.
D:
P:

14
B:
P:
M
P:
D:
P:

7
B:
P:
D:
P:

15
B:
P:
D:
P:

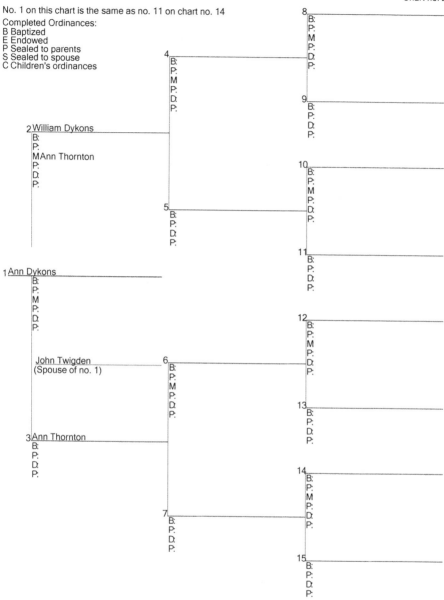

No. 1 on this chart is the same as no. 11 on chart no. 14

Completed Ordinances:
B Baptized
E Endowed
P Sealed to parents
S Sealed to spouse
C Children's ordinances

2 William Dykons
B:
P:
M Ann Thornton
P:
D:
P:

1 Ann Dykons
B:
P:
M
P:
D:
P:

John Twigden
(Spouse of no. 1)

3 Ann Thornton
B:
P:
D:
P:

4
B:
P:
M
P:
D:
P:

5
B:
P:
D:
P:

6
B:
P:
M
P:
D:
P:

7
B:
P:
D:
P:

8
B:
P:
M
P:
D:
P:

9
B:
P:
D:
P:

10
B:
P:
M
P:
D:
P:

11
B:
P:
D:
P:

12
B:
P:
M
P:
D:
P:

13
B:
P:
D:
P:

14
B:
P:
M
P:
D:
P:

15
B:
P:
D:
P:

Bob McDill

No. 1 on this chart is the same as no. 8 on chart no. 15

Completed Ordinances:
B Baptized
E Endowed
P Sealed to parents
S Sealed to spouse
C Children's ordinances

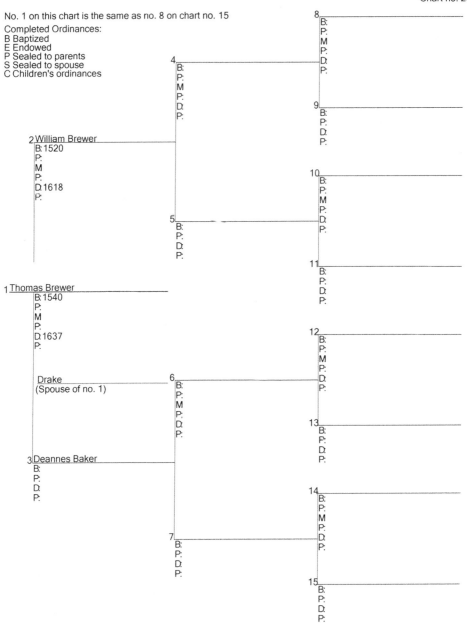

8
B:
P:
M
P:
D:
P:

4
B:
P:
M
P:
D:
P:

9
B:
P:
D:
P:

2 William Brewer
B: 1520
P:
M
P:
D. 1618
P:

10
B:
P:
M
P:
D:
P:

5
B:
P:
D:
P:

11
B:
P:
D:
P:

1 Thomas Brewer
B: 1540
P:
M
P:
D. 1637
P:

12
B:
P:
M
P:
D:
P:

Drake
(Spouse of no. 1)

6
B:
P:
M
P:
D:
P:

13
B:
P:
D:
P:

3 Deannes Baker
B:
P:
D:
P:

14
B:
P:
M
P:
D:
P:

7
B:
P:
D:
P:

15
B:
P:
D:
P:

The Ancestors and Descendants of Robert Nathaniel McDill

Pedigree Chart Index

Name	Born/Chr	Died/Bur	Found on Chart	Position
, Ann			10	5
, Ann (Skinner?)			15	3
, Caroline	1822		1	11
, Eleanor			12	7
, Elizabeth			6	9
, Elizabeth			5	9
, Elizabeth			7	3
, Elizabeth			6	5
, Francis			11	7
, Honor			10	3
, Joanna			4	3
, Lucreece			16	3
, Lucy			14	7
, Martha			8	11
, Mary			3	3
, Rose			18	7
, Sarah			11	11
, Usley			4	5
Dickens, William			24	2
(Meary), Mary	Abt 1740	Living 1790 Census	2	3
Aubrey, Dorothy			9	5
Aubrey, Richard			9	10
Baker, Deannes			25	3
Barwick, Elizabeth		3 Jun 1569	20	3
Beckwith, Grace	1576	1665	13	9
Brewer, Christiana	14 Mar 1827	14 Jun 1909	1	15
Brewer, George III	1718	1815	6	8
Brewer, George Jr.	1718	1761	11	2
Brewer, George G.	1685	1 Aug 1744	11	4
Brewer, John III	1635	1701	11	8
Brewer, John Jr.	1600	1669	15	2
Brewer, John	1565	1635	15	4
Brewer, Matthew	1774		6	4
Brewer, Thomas	1540	1637	15	8
Brewer, William	1520	1618	25	2
Brewer, Wyche	1798		6	2
Butler, John			23	4
Butler, Margaret	1568		14	9
Butler, William			23	2
Callaham, John	1734	Abt 1804	3	4

Name	Born/Chr	Died/Bur	Found on Chart	Position
Callaham, Morris	1755/1765	1823	3	2
Callaham, Nicholas	Bef 1693		3	8
Callaham, Samuel W.	1811	Bef 1900	1	10
Callahan, Sarah Elizabeth	14 Jul 1837	25 Sep 1933	1	5
Cloud, Isaac Jr.	Abt 1787	17 Aug 1855	4	2
Cloud, Isaac	1730/1755	Aft 1820	4	4
Cloud, James Madison	Abt 1817	1868	1	12
Cloud, Joseph	Abt 1725		4	8
Cloud, Lida Adelia	24 Jun 1877	19 Jun 1928	1	3
Cloud, Marquis Lafayette	22 Dec 1842	14 Aug 1903	1	6
Collett, Hanna		1653	16	5
Darnell, David			9	12
Darnell, Elizabeth			9	3
Darnell, Waugh			9	6
Deathick, Christian			18	3
Deathick, Simon			18	6
Dickens, Anne			14	11
Drake,			15	9
Garton, Catherine			8	5
Garton, John			8	10
Gleane, Mary		27 Jul 1631	12	5
Gleane, Sir Peter			12	10
Gleane, Thomas		1602	19	2
Greek, Margaret			23	3
Grimston, Anne			21	9
Grove, Mary			15	5
Grove, Ralph			15	10
Harbin, Ann			8	7
Harris, Anna	18 Jan 1798	13 Jun 1869	5	3
Harris, Sarah			5	7
King, Cecily			12	9
King, Margaret "Peggy"		1882	1	13
Lanier, Clement		1661	16	4
Lanier, John	1633		16	2
Lanier, John Jr.	1655	1719	11	10
Lanier, Nicholas			16	8
Lanier, Sarah	1686	1724-29	11	5
Leslie, Ann (Logan?)	1795	24 May 1872	1	9
Leslie, Janet (Jenet)			2	5
Light, Elizabeth	1547	1599	22	3
Light, Walter			22	6
Markham, Anne	1554	1618	21	3
McCauley, Ruby Lee	2 Jun 1915	3 Mar 2009	1	Spouse
McDill, Guy Vernon	7 May 1910	18 Dec 1973	1	1
McDill, John	1675	1761	2	4
McDill, Nathaniel I	1740	16 Apr 1785	2	2
McDill, Nathaniel II	1775	20 Jan 1857	1	8
McDill, Robert Nathaniel	8 Aug 1867	25 Aug 1960	1	2
McDill, Thomas Alexander	26 Nov 1826	23 Sep 1909	1	4
McPherson, Flora			6	3

Name	Born/Chr	Died/Bur	Found on Chart	Position
Meadord, Dorothy			9	11
Merriton, Ann	1605	18 Mar 1670	13	5
Moore, Elizabeth			8	3
Moore, Francis			8	6
Morris, Katherine			12	3
Morris, Major George		1685	12	6
Mottram, Ann	1639	1707	13	3
Mottram, Col. John			13	6
Pettit, Thomas	Abt 1665	17 May 1720	8	8
Pettit, Thomas Pettus aka	Abt 1609		12	2
Pettus, Thomas	Bap 17 Sep 1552	6 Jun 1660	12	8
Pettus, Thomas	1519	7 Jan 1597	18	2
Pettus, William	Bap 12 Aug 1583	19 Dec 1648	12	4
Petty, Henrietta Virginia	28 Jun 1848	13 Dec 1925	1	7
Petty, John Wright	28 Feb 1791	25 Sep 1876	5	2
Petty, John Wright II	12 Nov 1824	27 Mar 1858	1	14
Petty, Thomas	Abt 1680	1740/1750	8	4
Petty, Thomas	1704		8	2
Petty, William	Abt 1730	27 May 1805	5	8
Petty, William Eli	13 Mar 1764	26 Sep 1834	5	4
Pope, Anne		1668	14	3
Pope, Nathaniel	1610	Apr 1660	14	6
Saltinstall, Elizabeth			17	5
Saltinstall, Sir Richard			17	10
Suckling, Maude			12	11
Suckling, Robert		1589	20	2
Sutton, Margaret			23	5
Thornton, Ann			21	5
Thornton, Ann			24	3
Twigden, Amphillis	1599	1654/0055	14	5
Twigden, John		Nov 1610	14	10
Washington, Ann	Abt 1667	Bef 11 Mar 1698	9	9
Washington, Col, John	1627-30	1677	14	2
Washington, Lawrence	1602	21 Jan 1651	14	4
Washington, Lawrence	1566	1616	14	8
Washington, Robert	1544	1621-22	22	2
Weaver, John			7	2
Weaver, Joyce	Bef 1699		3	9
Williams, Ann	1735	1825	5	11
Williams, Jonas			10	4
Williams, Jonas II		1744	10	2
Wilson, Racheal			8	9
Wolmer, Alice			19	3
Woodward, Ursala			22	7
Wright, Captain Richard Whittington	1633	1663	13	2

Name	Born/Chr	Died/Bur	Found on Chart	Position
Wright, Francis III	1601	1655	13	4
Wright, Francis	1574	1623	21	2
Wright, Francis Jr.	1563	1651	13	8
Wright, John	Jun 1685	1759	9	4
Wright, John III	1731	30 Oct 1789	5	10
Wright, John II	Dec 1710	27 Feb 1792	9	2
Wright, Lucretia	16 Jul 1765	16 Aug 1842	5	5
Wright, Major Francis	Abt 1660	Jun 1713	9	8
Wright, Robert	1501	18 Jul 1594	21	8
Wright, William	1523	23 Aug 1621	21	4
Wyche, Abigail			11	3
Wyche, Henry Jr.	4 Nov 1645		11	12
Wyche, Henry III		1740	11	6
Wyche, Rev. Henry	1604	Aug 1672	17	2
Wyche, Richard	1554	1621	17	4
Wyche, Sir Hugh	1461		26	2
Wyche, Thomas			17	8

The Ancestors and Descendants of Robert Nathaniel McDill

Our Family

The Ancestors and Descendants of Robert Nathaniel McDill